The Oracle Database Blueprint: Your Path to Mastery

1. Introduction to Oracle Databases

- Overview of Oracle databases
- Importance in the enterprise world
- Goals of the book

2. Understanding Database Concepts

- What is a database?
- Key components of Oracle architecture
- Oracle database versions and features

3. Installation and Configuration

- Installing Oracle Database software
- Configuring Oracle instances
- Post-installation tasks

4. Oracle Database Architecture

- Physical and logical structures
- Memory architecture
- Process architecture
- Storage architecture

5. Creating and Managing Databases

- Creating an Oracle database
- Managing tablespaces, data files, and control files
- Using Oracle Managed Files (OMF)

6. User and Security Management

- Creating and managing users
- Roles and privileges
- Implementing security best practices

7. Oracle Networking

- Oracle Net Services overview
- Configuring listeners and services
- Advanced networking topics (e.g., Oracle Connection Manager)

8. SQL and PL/SQL Fundamentals

- Writing SQL queries
- Introduction to PL/SQL
- Stored procedures, functions, and triggers

9. Advanced SQL Techniques

- Query optimization
- Advanced joins, subqueries, and set operations
- Analytical functions and hierarchical queries

10. Data Modeling and Design

- Entity-Relationship (ER) modeling
- Normalization and denormalization
- Designing efficient schemas

11. Backup and Recovery Strategies

- Backup types and methods
- Using RMAN (Recovery Manager)
- Point-in-time recovery and flashback technologies

12. Performance Tuning and Optimization

- Performance tuning methodologies
- SQL query optimization techniques
- Monitoring and diagnosing performance issues

13. Oracle Data Pump and Export/Import Utilities

- Overview of Oracle Data Pump
- Export and import operations
- Best practices for data migration

14. High Availability and Disaster Recovery

- Oracle RAC (Real Application Clusters)
- Data Guard and standby databases
- Oracle GoldenGate for replication

15. Database Patching and Upgrading

- Applying patches and patch management
- Upgrading Oracle databases
- Rolling back patches

16. Oracle Cloud and Multitenant Architecture

- Introduction to Oracle Cloud services
- Configuring and managing Oracle databases in the cloud
- Multitenant architecture and pluggable databases

17. Oracle Enterprise Manager

- Overview of Oracle Enterprise Manager (OEM)
- Monitoring and managing databases with OEM
- Automating routine tasks

18. Data Warehousing and Big Data Integration

- Designing and implementing data warehouses
- ETL processes and tools
- Integrating Oracle with Big Data technologies

19. Advanced Security Features

- Transparent Data Encryption (TDE)
- Virtual Private Database (VPD)
- Data masking and redaction

20. Case Studies and Real-World Applications

- Real-world scenarios and solutions
- Troubleshooting common issues
- Best practices for Oracle database management

This structure covers fundamental and advanced topics, providing a comprehensive guide for readers to master Oracle Database.

Chapter 1: Introduction to Oracle Databases

1.1 What is an Oracle Database?

An Oracle database is a collection of data treated as a unit. The purpose of a database is to store and retrieve related information. Oracle Database is one of the most popular database management systems (DBMS) in the world, widely used in various industries due to its robustness, scalability, and comprehensive feature set.

Oracle databases are known for their ability to handle large volumes of data and support a wide range of applications. They are the backbone of many enterprise-level applications, supporting everything from transaction processing to data warehousing and business analytics.

1.2 The Evolution of Oracle Database

Oracle Corporation, founded in 1977 by Larry Ellison, Bob Miner, and Ed Oates, has been at the forefront of database technology innovation. The first version of Oracle Database, released in 1979, was the first commercially available SQL-based relational database management system (RDBMS). Since then, Oracle has continually evolved, introducing new features, improving performance, and adapting to the changing technological landscape.

Key milestones in Oracle's history include:

- **Oracle 7** (1992): Introduced PL/SQL, a procedural language extension for SQL, allowing developers to write complex queries and applications.

- **Oracle 8** (1997): Introduced support for large objects (LOBs) and partitioning, improving the handling of large datasets.
- **Oracle 9i** (2001): Introduced Real Application Clusters (RAC) for high availability and grid computing capabilities.
- **Oracle 10g** (2003): Focused on grid computing, allowing organizations to leverage clusters of low-cost servers.
- **Oracle 11g** (2007): Improved performance tuning, data compression, and introduced Active Data Guard for disaster recovery.
- **Oracle 12c** (2013): Introduced the multitenant architecture, allowing multiple pluggable databases within a single container database.
- **Oracle 19c** (2019): Brought enhancements in security, performance, and automated database management.

Understanding the history and evolution of Oracle Database helps in appreciating its current capabilities and the vision behind its development.

1.3 Key Features of Oracle Database

Oracle Database is renowned for its rich set of features, making it a preferred choice for enterprises. Some of the key features include:

- **Scalability and Performance:** Oracle Database can handle massive amounts of data and high transaction volumes without compromising performance. It supports both vertical and horizontal scaling,

allowing organizations to expand their database environments as needed.
- **High Availability:** Oracle offers robust high-availability solutions, including Real Application Clusters (RAC) and Data Guard. These features ensure that databases remain available even in the event of hardware failures or other disruptions.
- **Security:** Oracle Database provides advanced security features, including encryption, auditing, and data masking, to protect sensitive data. Oracle's Virtual Private Database (VPD) and Label Security further enhance data protection.
- **Comprehensive Management Tools:** Oracle Enterprise Manager (OEM) is a powerful tool for monitoring and managing Oracle databases. It provides a single interface for managing multiple databases, automating routine tasks, and optimizing performance.
- **Cloud Integration:** Oracle Database is fully integrated with Oracle Cloud, offering organizations the flexibility to deploy databases on-premises, in the cloud, or in a hybrid environment. Oracle's Autonomous Database, a cloud-based, self-managing database service, represents the latest innovation in database management.
- **Data Warehousing and Big Data Support:** Oracle Database supports advanced data warehousing capabilities, including partitioning, parallel processing, and materialized views. It also integrates with Big Data technologies, enabling organizations to analyze large volumes of unstructured data.

1.4 Why Learn Oracle Database?

Mastering Oracle Database is a valuable skill for IT professionals, developers, and database administrators (DBAs). Here are some reasons why learning Oracle Database is important:

- **Industry Demand:** Oracle Database is widely used in various industries, including finance, healthcare, telecommunications, and government. Knowledge of Oracle Database opens up numerous job opportunities.
- **Versatility:** Oracle Database is versatile and can be used for a wide range of applications, from small transactional systems to large data warehouses.
- **Career Advancement:** Becoming proficient in Oracle Database can lead to career advancement opportunities, including roles such as Oracle DBA, database architect, and database developer.
- **Community and Resources:** Oracle has a large, active community of users and developers. There are numerous resources available for learning, including official Oracle documentation, online courses, forums, and user groups.

1.5 Overview of the Book

This book, "The Oracle Database Blueprint: Your Path to Mastery," is designed to guide you through the process of mastering Oracle Database. Whether you are a beginner or an experienced professional, this book covers all the essential topics you need to become proficient in Oracle Database management.

The book is divided into 20 chapters, each focusing on a specific aspect of Oracle Database:

1. **Introduction to Oracle Databases**
2. **Understanding Database Concepts**
3. **Installation and Configuration**
4. **Oracle Database Architecture**
5. **Creating and Managing Databases**
6. **User and Security Management**
7. **Oracle Networking**
8. **SQL and PL/SQL Fundamentals**
9. **Advanced SQL Techniques**
10. **Data Modeling and Design**
11. **Backup and Recovery Strategies**
12. **Performance Tuning and Optimization**
13. **Oracle Data Pump and Export/Import Utilities**
14. **High Availability and Disaster Recovery**
15. **Database Patching and Upgrading**
16. **Oracle Cloud and Multitenant Architecture**
17. **Oracle Enterprise Manager**
18. **Data Warehousing and Big Data Integration**
19. **Advanced Security Features**
20. **Case Studies and Real-World Applications**

Each chapter is structured to provide a deep understanding of the topic, with practical examples, tips, and best practices. By the end of this book, you will have a solid foundation in Oracle Database and be well-equipped to manage and optimize Oracle environments in the real world.

1.6 Getting Started

To get the most out of this book, it is recommended that you have a basic understanding of databases and SQL. If you are new to databases, you may want to review some introductory materials on relational databases and SQL before diving into the technical chapters.

Throughout the book, you will find exercises and examples that you can try on your own. It is highly recommended to set up an Oracle Database environment where you can practice the concepts and techniques discussed in the book.

Let's begin your journey towards mastering Oracle Database!

Chapter 2: Understanding Database Concepts

2.1 What is a Database?

A database is a structured collection of data that can be easily accessed, managed, and updated. Databases are essential to modern computing as they allow us to store large amounts of information in an organized manner. At its core, a database is designed to manage and store data while ensuring that this data is available, consistent, and secure.

The data in a database is typically organized into tables, which consist of rows and columns. Each row in a table represents a unique record, and each column represents a specific attribute of that record. For example, in a customer database, a table might contain columns for customer ID, name, address, and phone number, with each row representing a different customer.

2.2 Types of Databases

There are several types of databases, each serving different purposes and use cases:

- **Relational Databases:** These are the most common type of databases, where data is organized into tables with rows and columns. Relationships between tables are established through keys, such as primary keys and foreign keys. SQL (Structured Query Language) is the standard language used to manage and query data in relational databases. Oracle Database is a prime example of a relational database.

- **NoSQL Databases:** These databases are designed to handle unstructured data, such as documents, key-value pairs, and graphs. They are often used in scenarios where traditional relational databases may struggle, such as with large-scale, distributed systems. Examples include MongoDB, Cassandra, and Redis.
- **Object-Oriented Databases:** These databases store data in the form of objects, similar to how data is handled in object-oriented programming languages like Java and C++. They are useful for applications that require complex data models and relationships. ObjectDB is an example of an object-oriented database.
- **Hierarchical Databases:** In these databases, data is organized in a tree-like structure, where each record has a parent-child relationship. IBM's Information Management System (IMS) is an example of a hierarchical database.
- **Graph Databases:** These databases use graph structures with nodes, edges, and properties to represent and store data. They are particularly useful for analyzing relationships in social networks, fraud detection, and recommendation engines. Neo4j is a well-known graph database.

Understanding the different types of databases helps in choosing the right database system based on the specific requirements of an application.

2.3 The Relational Database Model

The relational database model, introduced by E.F. Codd in 1970, revolutionized the way data is stored and managed. In this model, data is stored in tables (also called relations) that consist of rows and columns. The key components of the relational database model include:

- **Tables (Relations):** A table is a collection of related data entries and consists of rows and columns. Each table typically represents an entity, such as customers, orders, or products.
- **Rows (Tuples):** Each row in a table represents a single record, which is a specific instance of the entity. For example, in a customer table, each row would represent a different customer.
- **Columns (Attributes):** Columns represent the attributes of the entity, such as customer ID, name, and address in a customer table.
- **Primary Keys:** A primary key is a unique identifier for each record in a table. It ensures that each record can be uniquely identified and retrieved. For example, a customer ID column could be the primary key in a customer table.
- **Foreign Keys:** A foreign key is a column or set of columns in one table that references the primary key of another table. This establishes a relationship between the two tables, allowing for the creation of complex queries that join data from multiple tables.
- **SQL (Structured Query Language):** SQL is the standard language used to interact with relational databases. It allows users to create, read, update,

and delete data (often abbreviated as CRUD operations) as well as manage the database schema.

The relational model's emphasis on data integrity, normalization (the process of organizing data to minimize redundancy), and the ability to join tables to perform complex queries makes it ideal for many applications.

2.4 Oracle Database Architecture Overview

Oracle Database is built on a complex yet efficient architecture designed to manage data in a scalable, reliable, and secure manner. Understanding the basic components of Oracle Database architecture is crucial for anyone looking to master Oracle Database.

The architecture of Oracle Database can be divided into three main components:

- **1. Instance:** The instance is the set of memory structures and background processes that manage the database. The instance is responsible for handling user requests, reading and writing data to and from the database, and ensuring the database operates efficiently.
    - **Memory Structures:** The main memory structures in an Oracle instance include the System Global Area (SGA) and the Program Global Area (PGA). The SGA is a shared memory area used by all users connected to the database, while the PGA is a private memory area used by individual user processes.

- o **Background Processes:** Oracle Database uses various background processes to manage tasks such as writing data to disk, handling user connections, and recovering the database in case of failure. Some of the key background processes include DBWn (Database Writer), LGWR (Log Writer), and SMON (System Monitor).
- **2. Database:** The database is the actual data stored on disk. It consists of physical files, including data files, control files, and redo log files.
  - o **Data Files:** Data files contain the actual data stored in the database, including tables, indexes, and other objects. Data files are organized into logical storage units called tablespaces.
  - o **Control Files:** Control files store metadata about the database, such as the names and locations of data files, the state of the database, and the timestamps of the last backup.
  - o **Redo Log Files:** Redo log files record all changes made to the database. They are crucial for database recovery in case of a crash or other failures.
- **3. Schema Objects:** Schema objects are the logical structures that directly refer to the database's data. These objects include tables, indexes, views, sequences, and synonyms.
  - o **Tables:** Tables are the basic storage structure in a relational database. They store data in rows and columns.

- **Indexes:** Indexes are used to improve the speed of data retrieval by providing quick access to rows in a table.
- **Views:** Views are virtual tables based on the result of an SQL query. They do not store data themselves but provide a way to present data from one or more tables.
- **Sequences:** Sequences are used to generate unique numeric values, often used for primary key columns.
- **Synonyms:** Synonyms provide alternate names for database objects, making it easier to reference them in SQL statements.

2.5 Understanding SQL and PL/SQL

SQL (Structured Query Language) is the standard language used to interact with relational databases like Oracle. It allows users to perform various operations on the data stored in a database. The basic operations include:

- **SELECT:** Used to retrieve data from one or more tables.
- **INSERT:** Used to add new records to a table.
- **UPDATE:** Used to modify existing records in a table.
- **DELETE:** Used to remove records from a table.

In addition to these basic operations, SQL also provides commands for managing database objects, such as creating tables, altering table structures, and managing users and privileges.

PL/SQL (Procedural Language/SQL) is Oracle's procedural extension to SQL. It allows developers to write complex scripts that include control structures (such as loops and conditionals), exception handling, and the ability to define procedures, functions, and triggers. PL/SQL is essential for developing robust, high-performance database applications.

2.6 Normalization and Data Integrity

Normalization is the process of organizing data in a database to reduce redundancy and improve data integrity. The goal of normalization is to structure the database in such a way that each piece of data is stored only once, reducing the risk of inconsistencies.

Normalization typically involves dividing a large table into smaller tables and defining relationships between them using foreign keys. The process of normalization follows several steps, known as normal forms, each addressing specific types of redundancy and ensuring data integrity.

Data Integrity refers to the accuracy and consistency of data stored in a database. Oracle Database provides several mechanisms to enforce data integrity:

- **Primary Keys:** Ensure that each record in a table is unique.
- **Foreign Keys:** Maintain the referential integrity between tables by ensuring that a foreign key value always corresponds to a valid primary key value in the related table.
- **Check Constraints:** Ensure that data meets specific criteria before it is entered into a table.

- **Unique Constraints:** Ensure that all values in a column or a set of columns are unique across the table.

2.7 Summary

Understanding database concepts is fundamental to mastering Oracle Database. This chapter provided an overview of what a database is, the different types of databases, and the key concepts of the relational database model. We also explored the Oracle Database architecture, including its instance, database, and schema objects.

As we move forward, these foundational concepts will be essential as we delve into more advanced topics, such as installation, configuration, and database management. In the next chapter, we will explore how to install and configure an Oracle Database, setting the stage for hands-on learning and practical application.

Now that you have a solid understanding of database concepts, you're ready to start working with Oracle Database itself. Let's move on to installation and configuration in the next chapter!

Chapter 3: Installation and Configuration

3.1 Overview of Oracle Database Installation

Installing Oracle Database is the first step in setting up a robust and scalable database environment. This chapter will guide you through the installation process, covering the prerequisites, installation options, and configuration steps necessary to get Oracle Database up and running. Whether you're installing Oracle on a local machine for development or on a server for production, understanding the installation process is crucial for ensuring a smooth setup.

3.2 System Requirements and Prerequisites

Before installing Oracle Database, it is essential to ensure that your system meets the minimum hardware and software requirements. These requirements vary depending on the version of Oracle Database and the operating system you are using. Here are some general prerequisites:

- **Hardware Requirements:**
    - **Processor:** A modern multi-core processor with a clock speed of 2.0 GHz or higher.
    - **Memory:** At least 2 GB of RAM for a basic installation; more memory is recommended for production environments.
    - **Disk Space:** A minimum of 10 GB of free disk space for installation files and database storage. Production environments may

require significantly more space depending on the size of the database.
  - **Network:** A stable network connection if you plan to install Oracle Database on a remote server or configure it for network access.
- **Software Requirements:**
  - **Operating System:** Oracle Database supports various operating systems, including Oracle Linux, Red Hat Enterprise Linux, SUSE Linux Enterprise Server, Microsoft Windows, and Solaris. Ensure that your operating system version is supported by the Oracle Database version you are installing.
  - **Kernel Parameters:** On Linux systems, certain kernel parameters must be configured to meet Oracle's requirements. These include parameters for shared memory, semaphores, and file descriptors.
  - **Dependencies:** Certain libraries and packages must be installed on the system. For example, on Linux, you may need to install packages like glibc, libaio, and compat-libstdc++. On Windows, ensure that the Visual C++ Redistributable is installed.

3.3 Downloading Oracle Database Software

Oracle Database software is available for download from the Oracle Technology Network (OTN) website. Here's how you can download it:

1. **Visit the Oracle Technology Network:** Go to the Oracle Technology Network website (https://www.oracle.com/database/technologies/).
2. **Select the Database Version:** Choose the appropriate version of Oracle Database based on your requirements (e.g., Oracle 19c, Oracle 21c).
3. **Select the Operating System:** Choose the operating system on which you intend to install Oracle Database.
4. **Download the Installation Files:** Click on the download link to download the installation files. Depending on the version, this might be a single ZIP file or multiple files.

You may need to create a free Oracle account or sign in to an existing account to access the download. Once downloaded, extract the installation files to a directory on your system.

3.4 Oracle Installation Options

Oracle Database offers several installation options to cater to different use cases:

- **Enterprise Edition:** This edition includes all Oracle Database features, including advanced security, high availability, and management tools. It is ideal for large-scale, mission-critical applications.
- **Standard Edition:** This edition includes most of the core database features but omits some of the advanced options available in the Enterprise Edition. It is suitable for small to medium-sized businesses.
- **Express Edition (XE):** Oracle Database XE is a free, entry-level edition that includes a subset of the

features available in the Standard and Enterprise editions. It is ideal for learning, development, and small applications.
- **Personal Edition:** This edition is similar to the Enterprise Edition but is licensed for single-user development and personal use.
- **Cloud Edition:** Oracle also offers cloud-based deployment options through Oracle Cloud Infrastructure (OCI). The Autonomous Database services, such as Autonomous Data Warehouse (ADW) and Autonomous Transaction Processing (ATP), are fully managed services that eliminate the need for manual installation and management.

Depending on your needs, choose the appropriate edition for installation. For the purposes of this chapter, we will focus on installing the Enterprise Edition on a Linux system.

3.5 Installing Oracle Database on Linux

Installing Oracle Database on a Linux system involves several steps, including setting up the environment, running the Oracle Universal Installer (OUI), and performing post-installation tasks. Below is a detailed step-by-step guide:

Step 1: Prepare the System

1. **Update the System:** Before installation, ensure that your system is up to date by running the following command:

```
sudo yum update -y
```

2. **Install Required Packages:** Install the necessary packages and libraries using the package manager:

```
sudo yum install -y binutils compat-libcap1 gcc gcc-c++ glibc glibc-devel \
ksh libaio libaio-devel libX11 libXau libXi libXtst libXrender make \
sysstat
```

3. **Create Oracle User and Groups:** Create a user and groups for Oracle Database:

```
sudo groupadd oinstall
sudo groupadd dba
sudo useradd -g oinstall -G dba oracle
sudo passwd oracle
```

4. **Create Directories for Installation:** Create directories for the Oracle software and database files:

```
sudo mkdir -p /u01/app/oracle/product/19.0.0/dbhome_1
sudo mkdir -p /u02/oradata
sudo chown -R oracle:oinstall /u01 /u02
sudo chmod -R 775 /u01 /u02
```

5. **Configure Kernel Parameters:** Update the /etc/sysctl.conf file to include the following parameters:

```
fs.aio-max-nr = 1048576
fs.file-max = 6815744
kernel.shmall = 2097152
kernel.shmmax = 2147483648
kernel.shmmni = 4096
kernel.sem = 250 32000 100 128
net.ipv4.ip_local_port_range = 9000 65500
net.core.rmem_default = 262144
net.core.rmem_max = 4194304
net.core.wmem_default = 262144
net.core.wmem_max = 1048576
```

6. **Apply Kernel Parameter Changes:**

```
sudo sysctl -p
```

Step 2: Install Oracle Database

1. **Switch to the Oracle User:**

```
su - oracle
```

2. **Run the Oracle Universal Installer (OUI):** Navigate to the directory where you extracted the Oracle installation files and run the installer:

```
./runInstaller
```

3. **Follow the Installation Wizard:**
   - **Configure Security Updates:** You can choose whether to receive security updates from Oracle.
   - **Installation Option:** Select "Install database software only" if you plan to create the database manually later, or "Create and configure a database" to have the installer create a database for you.
   - **Installation Type:** Choose "Enterprise Edition."
   - **Installation Location:** Specify the Oracle base directory and the software location.
   - **Configuration:** Configure memory, character sets, and other database options.
   - **Perform Prerequisite Checks:** The installer will check your system for compatibility. Address any issues that arise.
   - **Install:** Click "Install" to begin the installation process. Monitor the progress and follow any prompts to complete the installation.
4. **Run the Root Scripts:** After the installation, you will be prompted to run root scripts. Open a new terminal window as the root user and run the following commands:

```
sudo /u01/app/oraInventory/orainstRoot.sh
sudo /u01/app/oracle/product/19.0.0/dbhome_1/root.sh
```

Step 3: Post-Installation Configuration

1. **Set Environment Variables:** Add the following lines to the .bash_profile file for the Oracle user:

   ```
   export ORACLE_BASE=/u01/app/oracle
   export ORACLE_HOME=$ORACLE_BASE/product/19.0.0/dbhome_1
   export ORACLE_SID=orcl
   export PATH=$PATH:$ORACLE_HOME/bin
   ```

   Apply the changes:

   ```
   source ~/.bash_profile
   ```

2. **Create a Listener:** Use Oracle Net Configuration Assistant (NETCA) to create and configure a listener:

   ```
   netca
   ```

   Follow the prompts to create a default listener.

3. **Verify the Installation:** Start the database and listener to verify that the installation was successful:

   ```
   lsnrctl start
   sqlplus / as sysdba
   startup
   ```

4. **Connect to the Database:** Connect to the database using SQL*Plus and perform a simple query to verify connectivity:

```
sqlplus system/password@localhost:1521/orcl
SELECT * FROM dual;
```

3.6 Oracle Database Configuration Assistant (DBCA)

The Oracle Database Configuration Assistant (DBCA) is a graphical tool that simplifies the process of creating, configuring, and managing Oracle databases. Here's how to use DBCA to create a new database:

1. **Launch DBCA:** Run the following command as the Oracle user:

```
dbca
```

2. **Create a Database:**
   - **Choose the Database Operation:** Select "Create a database."
   - **Select the Database Template:** Choose from predefined templates, such as "General Purpose" or "Data Warehouse."
   - **Configure Database Options:** Set options such as the database name, SID, character set, and memory configuration.

- **Specify Storage Options:** Choose between file system or Automatic Storage Management (ASM) for database storage.
- **Create Database:** Review the summary and click "Finish" to create the database.
3. **Manage Database:** After the database is created, you can use DBCA to manage database options, configure recovery settings, and manage database storage.

3.7 Oracle Enterprise Manager (OEM) Configuration

Oracle Enterprise Manager (OEM) is a web-based tool that provides a centralized interface for managing Oracle databases and related components. After installing Oracle Database, you can configure OEM to monitor and manage your database.

1. **Launch OEM Configuration:** During installation, you may be prompted to configure Oracle Enterprise Manager. If you skipped this step, you can configure it later using the following command:

```
emca -config dbcontrol db -repos create
```

2. **Access OEM:** Once configured, access Oracle Enterprise Manager by navigating to the following URL in your web browser:

```
https://<hostname>:5500/em
```

3. **Log in:** Log in using the SYS or SYSTEM user credentials. You will have access to a range of management tools for database performance monitoring, backup and recovery, and security management.

3.8 Post-Installation Tasks

After the installation and initial configuration, there are several post-installation tasks to consider:

- **Security Configuration:** Configure user accounts, roles, and privileges to secure the database. Oracle Database provides a range of security features, including encryption, auditing, and password policies.
- **Backup and Recovery Configuration:** Set up regular backups using Oracle Recovery Manager (RMAN) or Data Pump to ensure data is protected in case of failure.
- **Performance Tuning:** Monitor and optimize database performance using tools such as Oracle Automatic Workload Repository (AWR) and SQL Tuning Advisor.
- **Patching and Updates:** Regularly apply patches and updates from Oracle to keep your database secure and up to date. Use Oracle's OPatch utility to apply patches.

3.9 Summary

In this chapter, we explored the installation and configuration of Oracle Database. We covered the system requirements, installation options, and detailed steps for installing Oracle Database on a Linux system. Additionally, we discussed the use of Oracle tools such as DBCA and OEM for database management.

Installing and configuring Oracle Database is a critical first step in setting up a reliable and scalable database environment. With Oracle Database installed and configured, you are now ready to begin working with the database, managing data, and optimizing performance.

In the next chapter, we will dive into the basics of SQL and PL/SQL, providing you with the foundational skills needed to interact with Oracle Database and develop database applications.

Chapter 4: Understanding SQL and PL/SQL

4.1 Introduction to SQL

Structured Query Language (SQL) is the standard language for interacting with relational databases, including Oracle Database. SQL allows you to perform various operations on the data stored in a database, such as querying, inserting, updating, and deleting records. This chapter will introduce you to the fundamentals of SQL, focusing on how to use SQL to work with Oracle Database effectively.

4.2 SQL Data Types

SQL data types define the kind of data that can be stored in a database column. Understanding these data types is essential for designing tables and writing queries. Some of the most commonly used data types in Oracle SQL include:

- **CHAR(n):** Fixed-length character data, where n specifies the length.
- **VARCHAR2(n):** Variable-length character data, where n specifies the maximum length.
- **NUMBER(p,s):** Numeric data, where p specifies the precision and s specifies the scale.
- **DATE:** Date and time data.
- **BLOB:** Binary Large Object, used for storing binary data such as images or videos.
- **CLOB:** Character Large Object, used for storing large text data.

When creating a table, you must specify the data type for each column, ensuring that the data stored in the column is consistent and accurate.

4.3 Creating and Managing Tables

Tables are the fundamental structures used to store data in a relational database. In this section, we will explore how to create, alter, and drop tables in Oracle Database.

Creating a Table:

To create a table in Oracle Database, you use the CREATE TABLE statement. Here's an example:

```sql
CREATE TABLE employees (
    employee_id NUMBER(6) PRIMARY KEY,
    first_name VARCHAR2(50),
    last_name VARCHAR2(50),
    email VARCHAR2(100) UNIQUE,
    hire_date DATE,
    salary NUMBER(8,2)
);
```

In this example, the employees table is created with six columns: employee_id, first_name, last_name, email, hire_date, and salary. The employee_id column is designated as the primary key, meaning it uniquely identifies each record in the table.

Altering a Table:

If you need to modify an existing table, such as adding a new column or changing the data type of a column, you use the ALTER TABLE statement. For example, to add a new column called department_id to the employees table, you would use the following SQL statement:

```
ALTER TABLE employees
ADD department_id NUMBER(4);
```

Dropping a Table:

If you no longer need a table, you can remove it from the database using the DROP TABLE statement:

```
DROP TABLE employees;
```

This command permanently deletes the employees table and all of its data from the database.

4.4 Inserting, Updating, and Deleting Data

Once you have created a table, you can insert, update, and delete data within it. These operations are fundamental to maintaining the integrity and accuracy of the data stored in the database.

Inserting Data:

To insert a new record into a table, you use the INSERT INTO statement. Here's an example of how to insert a new employee record into the employees table:

```
INSERT INTO employees (employee_id, first_name, last_name, email, hire_date, salary)
VALUES (1001, 'John', 'Doe', 'johndoe@example.com', '01-SEP-2024', 50000);
```

This statement inserts a new employee with the specified details into the employees table.

Updating Data:

If you need to modify an existing record, you use the UPDATE statement. For example, to update the salary of the employee with employee_id 1001, you would use the following SQL statement:

```
UPDATE employees
SET salary = 55000
WHERE employee_id = 1001;
```

This command updates the salary of the specified employee to 55,000.

Deleting Data:

To remove a record from a table, you use the DELETE FROM statement. For example, to delete the employee with employee_id 1001, you would use the following SQL statement:

```
DELETE FROM employees
WHERE employee_id = 1001;
```

This statement deletes the specified employee from the employees table.

4.5 Querying Data with SELECT

The SELECT statement is one of the most powerful and commonly used SQL commands. It allows you to retrieve data from one or more tables in the database. In this section, we will explore the basics of querying data with SELECT.

Basic SELECT Statement:

The simplest form of the SELECT statement retrieves all columns and rows from a table:

```
SELECT * FROM employees;
```

This query returns all records and columns from the employees table.

Selecting Specific Columns:

If you only want to retrieve specific columns, you can list them in the SELECT statement:

```
SELECT first_name, last_name, email FROM employees;
```

This query returns only the first_name, last_name, and email columns for all employees.

Filtering Results with WHERE:

To filter the results of a query based on specific conditions, you use the WHERE clause. For example, to retrieve employees with a salary greater than 50,000, you would use the following query:

```
SELECT first_name, last_name, salary
FROM employees
WHERE salary > 50000;
```

This query returns only those employees whose salary is greater than 50,000.

Sorting Results with ORDER BY:

The ORDER BY clause allows you to sort the results of a query. For example, to sort employees by their last name in ascending order, you would use the following query:

```
SELECT first_name, last_name, salary
FROM employees
ORDER BY last_name ASC;
```

This query returns the employees sorted by last name in alphabetical order.

Grouping Results with GROUP BY:

The GROUP BY clause is used to group rows that share the same values in specified columns. It is often used with aggregate functions such as COUNT, SUM, AVG, MAX, and MIN. For example, to find the total salary for each department, you would use the following query:

```
SELECT department_id, SUM(salary) AS total_salary
FROM employees
GROUP BY department_id;
```

This query groups employees by department_id and calculates the total salary for each department.

4.6 Introduction to PL/SQL

PL/SQL (Procedural Language/SQL) is Oracle's procedural extension of SQL. It allows you to write code that combines SQL statements with procedural logic, such as loops and conditionals. PL/SQL is used to create stored procedures, functions, triggers, and packages, which can be stored and executed within the database.

Basic Structure of PL/SQL:

A basic PL/SQL block consists of the following sections:

1. **Declaration Section:** Here, you declare variables, constants, and other data structures.
2. **Executable Section:** This section contains the procedural code, including SQL statements and control structures.
3. **Exception Handling Section:** This optional section handles exceptions or errors that may occur during execution.

Here's an example of a simple PL/SQL block:

```
DECLARE
  v_employee_id employees.employee_id%TYPE := 1001;
  v_salary employees.salary%TYPE;
BEGIN
  SELECT salary INTO v_salary
  FROM employees
  WHERE employee_id = v_employee_id;

  IF v_salary < 60000 THEN
    UPDATE employees
    SET salary = salary + 5000
    WHERE employee_id = v_employee_id;
  END IF;

  COMMIT;
EXCEPTION
  WHEN NO_DATA_FOUND THEN
    DBMS_OUTPUT.PUT_LINE('Employee not found.');
  WHEN OTHERS THEN
    DBMS_OUTPUT.PUT_LINE('An error occurred.');
END;
```

In this example:

- The **Declaration Section** declares variables v_employee_id and v_salary.
- The **Executable Section** retrieves the salary of the specified employee, checks if it is less than 60,000, and increases the salary by 5,000 if the condition is met.
- The **Exception Handling Section** handles any exceptions that occur, such as NO_DATA_FOUND.

Benefits of PL/SQL:

- **Tight Integration with SQL:** PL/SQL is fully integrated with SQL, allowing you to embed SQL statements directly within PL/SQL code.
- **Improved Performance:** PL/SQL allows for batch processing and reduces the number of network round-trips between the application and the database.
- **Modularity:** PL/SQL supports the creation of reusable modules such as procedures, functions, and packages, improving code maintainability.

4.7 Stored Procedures and Functions

Stored procedures and functions are subprograms that are stored in the database and can be reused multiple times. They encapsulate business logic and can be called from other PL/SQL blocks, triggers, or client applications.

Creating a Stored Procedure:

A stored procedure is created using the CREATE PROCEDURE statement. Here's an example:

```
CREATE OR REPLACE PROCEDURE increase_salary (
  p_employee_id IN employees.employee_id%TYPE,
  p_increase_amount IN NUMBER
)
IS
BEGIN
  UPDATE employees
  SET salary = salary + p_increase_amount
  WHERE employee_id = p_employee_id;

  COMMIT;
END;
```

This procedure takes two parameters: p_employee_id and p_increase_amount. It increases the salary of the specified employee by the specified amount.

Creating a Function:

A function is similar to a procedure but returns a value. Here's an example of creating a function that calculates the annual salary of an employee:

```sql
CREATE OR REPLACE FUNCTION calculate_annual_salary (
  p_employee_id IN employees.employee_id%TYPE
) RETURN NUMBER
IS
  v_salary employees.salary%TYPE;
  v_annual_salary NUMBER;
BEGIN
  SELECT salary INTO v_salary
  FROM employees
  WHERE employee_id = p_employee_id;

  v_annual_salary := v_salary * 12;

  RETURN v_annual_salary;
END;
```

This function takes an employee ID as a parameter and returns the employee's annual salary.

4.8 Summary

In this chapter, we covered the fundamentals of SQL and PL/SQL, essential tools for interacting with Oracle Database. We began by exploring SQL data types, creating and managing tables, and performing basic data operations such as inserting, updating, and deleting records. We also learned how to query data using the SELECT statement, with options for filtering, sorting, and grouping results.

The chapter then introduced PL/SQL, Oracle's procedural extension to SQL, highlighting its structure, benefits, and use in creating stored procedures and functions.

Mastering SQL and PL/SQL is crucial for effectively working with Oracle Database, as these languages allow you to manage data and implement business logic within the database. In the next chapter, we will delve into advanced SQL techniques, including joins, subqueries, and set operations, to further enhance your ability to interact with and manipulate data in Oracle Database.

Chapter 5: Advanced SQL Techniques

5.1 Understanding Joins

Joins are used to combine rows from two or more tables based on a related column between them. Joins are essential for querying data that is distributed across multiple tables. This section will cover the various types of joins available in SQL and how to use them effectively.

1. Inner Join:

The INNER JOIN clause returns only the rows where there is a match in both joined tables. It is the most commonly used join type. Here's an example of an inner join:

```sql
SELECT e.employee_id, e.first_name, d.department_name
FROM employees e
INNER JOIN departments d ON e.department_id = d.department_id;
```

In this query, we join the employees table with the departments table based on the department_id column. Only employees who have a corresponding department will be returned.

2. Left Join (or Left Outer Join):

The LEFT JOIN (or LEFT OUTER JOIN) returns all rows from the left table and the matched rows from the right table. If there is no match, the result is NULL on the right side. Here's an example:

```
SELECT e.employee_id, e.first_name, d.department_name
FROM employees e
LEFT JOIN departments d ON e.department_id = d.department_id;
```

This query returns all employees and their corresponding department names. Employees without a department will still be included, with NULL in the department_name column.

3. Right Join (or Right Outer Join):

The RIGHT JOIN (or RIGHT OUTER JOIN) returns all rows from the right table and the matched rows from the left table. If there is no match, the result is NULL on the left side. Here's an example:

```
SELECT e.employee_id, e.first_name, d.department_name
FROM employees e
RIGHT JOIN departments d ON e.department_id = d.department_id;
```

This query returns all departments and their corresponding employees. Departments without employees will still be included, with NULL in the employee_id and first_name columns.

4. Full Join (or Full Outer Join):

The FULL JOIN (or FULL OUTER JOIN) returns all rows when there is a match in either the left or right table. Rows that do not have a match in one of the tables will have NULL values for columns from that table. Here's an example:

```sql
SELECT e.employee_id, e.first_name, d.department_name
FROM employees e
FULL OUTER JOIN departments d ON e.department_id = d.department_id;
```

This query returns all employees and departments, including those that do not have a corresponding match in the other table.

5. Self Join:

A self-join is a regular join but the table is joined with itself. It is useful for querying hierarchical data or comparing rows within the same table. Here's an example:

```sql
SELECT e1.employee_id, e1.first_name AS employee, e2.first_name AS manager
FROM employees e1
INNER JOIN employees e2 ON e1.manager_id = e2.employee_id;
```

In this query, we join the employees table with itself to find each employee's manager.

5.2 Using Subqueries

A subquery, also known as an inner query or nested query, is a query within another query. Subqueries can be used in various parts of a SQL statement, such as the SELECT, WHERE, and HAVING clauses.

1. Subquery in the SELECT Clause:

Subqueries can be used to retrieve values for use in the main query. For example, to find employees with salaries greater than the average salary:

```
SELECT employee_id, first_name, salary
FROM employees
WHERE salary > (SELECT AVG(salary) FROM employees);
```

Here, the subquery calculates the average salary, and the main query retrieves employees earning more than that average.

2. Subquery in the WHERE Clause:

Subqueries in the WHERE clause can filter results based on conditions derived from another query. For example, to find employees who work in departments with more than 10 employees:

```
SELECT employee_id, first_name, department_id
FROM employees
WHERE department_id IN (SELECT department_id
        FROM employees
        GROUP BY department_id
        HAVING COUNT(*) > 10);
```

In this query, the subquery identifies departments with more than 10 employees, and the main query retrieves employees from those departments.

3. Correlated Subqueries:

A correlated subquery is a subquery that references columns from the outer query. It executes once for each row processed by the outer query. For example:

```
SELECT e1.employee_id, e1.first_name, e1.salary
FROM employees e1
WHERE e1.salary > (SELECT AVG(salary)
        FROM employees e2
        WHERE e1.department_id = e2.department_id);
```

In this query, the subquery calculates the average salary for the same department as each employee in the outer query.

5.3 Set Operations

Set operations allow you to combine the results of two or more queries. The result of a set operation is a single result set that includes the combined results of the individual queries. The most common set operations are UNION, INTERSECT, and EXCEPT (or MINUS in Oracle).

1. UNION:

The UNION operator combines the results of two queries and removes duplicate rows. Here's an example:

```
SELECT employee_id FROM employees
UNION
SELECT manager_id FROM managers;
```

This query retrieves a list of unique employee IDs and manager IDs.

2. INTERSECT:

The INTERSECT operator returns only the rows that are present in both result sets. Here's an example:

```
SELECT employee_id FROM employees
INTERSECT
SELECT employee_id FROM contractors;
```

This query retrieves employee IDs that are both in the employees and contractors tables.

3. EXCEPT (MINUS in Oracle):

The EXCEPT operator (or MINUS in Oracle) returns rows from the first result set that are not present in the second result set. Here's an example:

```
SELECT employee_id FROM employees
MINUS
SELECT employee_id FROM terminated_employees;
```

This query retrieves employee IDs that are not in the terminated_employees table.

5.4 Using Window Functions

Window functions provide an advanced way to perform calculations across a set of table rows that are related to the current row. Unlike aggregate functions, which return a single result for each group, window functions return a result for each row while considering other rows in the dataset.

1. ROW_NUMBER():

The ROW_NUMBER() function assigns a unique number to each row within a result set based on the specified ordering:

```
SELECT employee_id, first_name, salary,
    ROW_NUMBER() OVER (ORDER BY salary DESC) AS rank
FROM employees;
```

This query assigns a rank to each employee based on their salary, with the highest salary receiving rank 1.

2. RANK():

The RANK() function provides a rank to each row within the result set, with gaps in ranking for ties:

```
SELECT employee_id, first_name, salary,
    RANK() OVER (ORDER BY salary DESC) AS rank
FROM employees;
```

This query ranks employees based on their salary, with the same rank assigned to employees with the same salary.

3. DENSE_RANK():

The DENSE_RANK() function is similar to RANK(), but it does not leave gaps between ranks:

```
SELECT employee_id, first_name, salary,
    DENSE_RANK() OVER (ORDER BY salary DESC) AS rank
FROM employees;
```

This query ranks employees with no gaps in ranking, even for ties.

4. SUM() OVER():

The SUM() function can be used as a window function to calculate cumulative totals:

```
SELECT employee_id, first_name, salary,
    SUM(salary) OVER (ORDER BY hire_date) AS cumulative_salary
FROM employees;
```

This query calculates a running total of salaries ordered by the hire date.

5.5 Using Common Table Expressions (CTEs)

Common Table Expressions (CTEs) provide a way to create temporary result sets that can be referenced within a SELECT, INSERT, UPDATE, or DELETE statement. CTEs improve query readability and can simplify complex queries.

1. Basic CTE:

Here's an example of a basic CTE that calculates the average salary:

```sql
WITH avg_salary AS (
    SELECT AVG(salary) AS average
    FROM employees
)
SELECT employee_id, first_name, salary
FROM employees
WHERE salary > (SELECT average FROM avg_salary);
```

In this example, the avg_salary CTE calculates the average salary, and the main query retrieves employees earning more than that average.

2. Recursive CTE:

A recursive CTE is used to query hierarchical data, such as organizational structures. Here's an example:

```sql
WITH RECURSIVE org_chart (employee_id, manager_id, level) AS (
    SELECT employee_id, manager_id, 1
    FROM employees
    WHERE manager_id IS NULL
    UNION ALL
    SELECT e.employee_id, e.manager_id, oc.level + 1
    FROM employees e
    INNER JOIN org_chart oc ON e.manager_id = oc.employee_id
)
SELECT employee_id, manager_id, level
FROM org_chart;
```

In this example, the org_chart CTE recursively retrieves employees and their levels in the organizational hierarchy.

5.6 Summary

In this chapter, we explored advanced SQL techniques, including joins, subqueries, set operations, window functions, and common table expressions. Mastering these techniques is crucial for writing complex queries, optimizing performance, and effectively working with relational data.

Understanding and applying these advanced SQL features will enhance your ability to retrieve and manipulate data in Oracle Database, providing you with powerful tools for data analysis and reporting. In the next chapter, we will delve into database performance tuning and optimization, focusing on techniques and best practices to ensure your database operates efficiently and effectively.

Chapter 6: Database Performance Tuning and Optimization

6.1 Introduction to Performance Tuning

Database performance tuning is the process of optimizing the performance of a database system to ensure efficient operation and response times. Effective performance tuning involves identifying bottlenecks, optimizing queries, and configuring database settings to achieve the best possible performance. This chapter will cover key concepts and techniques for tuning and optimizing Oracle Database.

6.2 Understanding Performance Metrics

Before diving into performance tuning, it's essential to understand the key metrics used to evaluate database performance:

1. Response Time: The time it takes for the database to process a query and return the results. Reducing response time improves user experience and system efficiency.

2. Throughput: The number of transactions or queries processed by the database per unit of time. Higher throughput indicates better performance and capacity.

3. Resource Utilization: The amount of CPU, memory, and I/O resources used by the database. Efficient resource utilization ensures that the database operates within acceptable limits and avoids contention.

4. Wait Events: Events that occur when the database is waiting for resources, such as I/O operations or locks. Analyzing wait events helps identify performance bottlenecks.

6.3 Identifying Performance Bottlenecks

To optimize performance, you first need to identify the sources of performance issues. Common performance bottlenecks include:

1. Slow Queries: Queries that take a long time to execute due to inefficient execution plans, large datasets, or complex joins.

2. High CPU Usage: Excessive CPU consumption caused by inefficient queries, inadequate indexing, or high concurrency.

3. Disk I/O Bottlenecks: Slow disk I/O operations due to insufficient disk speed, high volume of read/write operations, or disk fragmentation.

4. Contention for Resources: Competition for database resources, such as locks or memory, which can lead to delays and reduced performance.

5. Memory Leaks: Issues where memory is not released properly, leading to excessive memory usage and potential system crashes.

6.4 Optimizing SQL Queries

Optimizing SQL queries is a critical aspect of performance tuning. Effective optimization techniques include:

1. Query Optimization Techniques:

- **Use Proper Indexes:** Indexes speed up query performance by allowing faster data retrieval. Analyze query execution plans to determine which columns should be indexed.
- **Avoid Full Table Scans:** Full table scans can be slow for large tables. Use indexes and write queries to avoid full table scans when possible.
- **Rewrite Complex Queries:** Simplify complex queries by breaking them into smaller, more manageable parts. Avoid nested queries when a join or a simpler query can achieve the same result.
- **Use EXISTS Instead of IN:** In some cases, using EXISTS can be more efficient than IN for subqueries, especially with large datasets.

2. Analyzing Execution Plans:

Execution plans show how Oracle Database executes a query. Analyzing execution plans helps identify inefficiencies and areas for optimization:

- **Use EXPLAIN PLAN:** The EXPLAIN PLAN statement provides a detailed execution plan for a query. Analyze the output to understand the query execution steps and identify potential issues.

- **Use Oracle SQL Developer:** SQL Developer offers a graphical interface to view and analyze execution plans. Use it to visualize query execution and identify optimization opportunities.

3. Optimizing Indexes:

Proper indexing improves query performance by reducing the amount of data scanned:

- **Create Indexes on Frequently Queried Columns:** Identify columns used in WHERE, JOIN, and ORDER BY clauses, and create indexes to speed up these operations.
- **Use Composite Indexes:** Composite indexes (indexes on multiple columns) can improve performance for queries that filter on multiple columns.
- **Monitor Index Usage:** Regularly review index usage to ensure that indexes are being used effectively. Remove unused or redundant indexes to reduce overhead.

6.5 Configuring Database Parameters

Database parameters control various aspects of Oracle Database performance. Proper configuration of these parameters is essential for optimal performance:

1. Memory Configuration:

- **Adjust SGA (System Global Area) and PGA (Program Global Area):** Configure the size of the SGA and PGA to ensure sufficient memory for caching data and

managing database operations. Use Oracle's Automatic Memory Management (AMM) feature to dynamically adjust memory settings.
- **Optimize Buffer Cache Size:** The buffer cache stores frequently accessed data blocks. Adjust the size of the buffer cache to balance memory usage and performance.

2. I/O Configuration:

- **Use Oracle Automatic Storage Management (ASM):** ASM simplifies and optimizes storage management by providing features like striping and mirroring.
- **Monitor Disk I/O Performance:** Use tools such as Oracle Enterprise Manager to monitor disk I/O performance and identify bottlenecks.

3. Concurrent Users and Sessions:

- **Configure Maximum Number of Sessions:** Set appropriate limits for the maximum number of concurrent database sessions to prevent resource contention.
- **Manage Connection Pooling:** Use connection pooling to manage database connections efficiently and reduce overhead.

6.6 Using Oracle Performance Tools

Oracle provides various tools to help monitor and optimize database performance:

1. Oracle Automatic Workload Repository (AWR):

AWR collects performance statistics and diagnostic information. Use AWR reports to analyze database performance over time and identify trends and issues.

2. Oracle SQL Tuning Advisor:

SQL Tuning Advisor provides recommendations for optimizing SQL queries based on execution plans and performance statistics.

3. Oracle Enterprise Manager (OEM):

OEM offers a comprehensive set of tools for monitoring, managing, and tuning Oracle Database. Use OEM to track performance metrics, analyze wait events, and generate performance reports.

4. Oracle Real-Time SQL Monitoring:

Real-Time SQL Monitoring provides real-time visibility into the performance of long-running SQL queries. Use it to identify and resolve performance issues during query execution.

6.7 Implementing Database Maintenance

Regular database maintenance is crucial for ensuring long-term performance and stability:

1. Regular Backups:

- **Perform Routine Backups:** Schedule regular backups to protect data and ensure recovery in case of failure. Use Oracle Recovery Manager (RMAN) for automated and efficient backup management.

2. Database Statistics:

- **Update Statistics Regularly:** Update database statistics to ensure the optimizer has accurate information for query planning. Use the DBMS_STATS package to gather and update statistics.

3. Monitor and Resolve Fragmentation:

- **Monitor Table and Index Fragmentation:** Fragmentation can impact performance. Use tools like Oracle's DBMS_REDEFINITION package to manage and reduce fragmentation.

6.8 Summary

In this chapter, we explored database performance tuning and optimization techniques for Oracle Database. We covered key performance metrics, identified common bottlenecks, and provided strategies for optimizing SQL queries, configuring database parameters, and using performance tools. Regular maintenance and effective use of Oracle's performance tools are essential for maintaining optimal database performance.

By mastering these performance tuning techniques, you can ensure that your Oracle Database operates efficiently and meets the demands of your applications and users. In the next chapter, we will explore database security practices and best practices to protect your Oracle Database from unauthorized access and data breaches.

Chapter 7: Database Security Practices

7.1 Introduction to Database Security

Database security is critical for protecting sensitive data and ensuring the integrity, availability, and confidentiality of your Oracle Database. Security measures help prevent unauthorized access, data breaches, and other threats that could compromise your database environment. This chapter will cover key security practices and features to secure your Oracle Database.

7.2 Understanding Security Threats

To effectively secure your database, it's important to understand common security threats:

1. Unauthorized Access: Access by individuals who should not have permission to view or modify data. This can result from weak authentication or improper access controls.

2. SQL Injection: A type of attack where malicious SQL code is injected into a query, potentially allowing attackers to manipulate or access data.

3. Data Breaches: Unauthorized access to sensitive or confidential data, which can lead to data theft or exposure.

4. Insider Threats: Risks from individuals within the organization who misuse their access to the database.

5. Denial of Service (DoS) Attacks: Attempts to disrupt the normal functioning of the database, often by overwhelming it with excessive requests.

7.3 Implementing Authentication and Authorization

1. Authentication:

Authentication is the process of verifying the identity of users accessing the database. Oracle Database supports various authentication methods:

- **Username and Password:** Basic authentication using a username and password. Ensure passwords are strong and regularly updated.
- **Oracle Advanced Security (OAS):** Provides additional authentication options, including Kerberos and LDAP-based authentication.
- **Single Sign-On (SSO):** Allows users to authenticate once and gain access to multiple systems without re-entering credentials.

2. Authorization:

Authorization controls what authenticated users can do within the database. Key practices include:

- **Role-Based Access Control (RBAC):** Assign roles to users based on their job functions. Roles define the permissions and privileges granted to users.
- **Least Privilege Principle:** Grant users the minimum permissions necessary to perform their tasks. Avoid providing unnecessary access that could be misused.

- **Privilege Management:** Regularly review and adjust user privileges. Use Oracle's GRANT and REVOKE statements to manage permissions.

7.4 Implementing Data Encryption

Encryption protects data by converting it into a format that is unreadable without the proper decryption key. Oracle provides several encryption options:

1. Transparent Data Encryption (TDE):

TDE encrypts data at rest, including database files and backups, without requiring changes to applications. It uses encryption keys stored in an external key management system.

2. Data Redaction:

Data Redaction masks sensitive data in query results to prevent unauthorized users from viewing it. Redaction policies can be applied to specific columns or data types.

3. Network Encryption:

Oracle supports encrypting data transmitted over the network using Secure Sockets Layer (SSL) or Transport Layer Security (TLS) protocols. This ensures data is protected during transmission.

7.5 Implementing Auditing and Monitoring

Auditing and monitoring are crucial for detecting and responding to security incidents:

1. Database Auditing:

Oracle Database includes auditing features to track database activities and user actions:

- **Standard Auditing:** Records events such as login attempts, SQL statements, and privilege changes. Configure standard auditing using the AUDIT statement.
- **Fine-Grained Auditing (FGA):** Provides detailed auditing capabilities for specific database operations and conditions. Use the DBMS_FGA package to create and manage FGA policies.

2. Monitoring Tools:

Use Oracle's monitoring tools to detect and respond to security threats:

- **Oracle Enterprise Manager (OEM):** Provides comprehensive monitoring and alerting features. Use OEM to track security-related events and performance metrics.
- **Oracle Data Guard:** Monitors and manages standby databases for data protection and disaster recovery.

7.6 Managing Database Security Configurations

1. Security Patches and Updates:

Regularly apply security patches and updates to protect against known vulnerabilities. Oracle regularly releases security patches through Critical Patch Updates (CPUs).

2. Configuring Security Policies:

Implement security policies to enforce best practices:

- **Password Policies:** Define password complexity, expiration, and history requirements to enhance security.
- **Account Lockout Policies:** Configure policies to lock accounts after a specified number of failed login attempts to prevent brute-force attacks.

3. Data Masking:

Data masking techniques anonymize sensitive data in non-production environments. This allows development and testing activities without exposing real data.

7.7 Backing Up and Recovering Data

Proper backup and recovery procedures are essential for protecting data and ensuring business continuity:

1. Backup Strategies:

- **Full Backups:** Regularly create full backups of the entire database to ensure complete data recovery.
- **Incremental Backups:** Perform incremental backups to capture changes since the last backup. This reduces backup time and storage requirements.
- **Backup Testing:** Regularly test backups to ensure they are complete and can be restored successfully.

2. Recovery Procedures:

- **Point-in-Time Recovery:** Restore the database to a specific point in time to recover from data corruption or accidental changes.
- **Disaster Recovery Planning:** Develop and implement a disaster recovery plan to ensure quick recovery in case of major incidents.

7.8 Best Practices for Database Security

1. Regular Security Reviews:

Conduct regular security reviews and assessments to identify and address vulnerabilities. Include periodic security audits and penetration testing.

2. Security Training:

Provide security training for database administrators and users to raise awareness of security best practices and threats.

3. Documentation and Policies:

Maintain up-to-date documentation of security policies, procedures, and configurations. Ensure that security practices are consistently applied and enforced.

7.9 Summary

In this chapter, we covered essential database security practices for protecting Oracle Database. We discussed understanding security threats, implementing authentication and authorization, data encryption, auditing and monitoring, security configurations, backup and recovery, and best practices.

By following these security practices, you can safeguard your Oracle Database against unauthorized access, data breaches, and other threats. In the next chapter, we will explore database backup and recovery techniques, focusing on strategies and tools to ensure data integrity and availability in case of failures or disasters.

Chapter 8: Database Backup and Recovery

8.1 Introduction to Backup and Recovery

Backup and recovery are fundamental aspects of database management that ensure data integrity and availability in the event of system failures, data corruption, or disasters. Effective backup and recovery strategies protect against data loss and enable quick restoration of database operations. This chapter will cover Oracle Database backup and recovery techniques, tools, and best practices.

8.2 Backup Strategies

1. Types of Backups:

Understanding the types of backups is crucial for developing an effective backup strategy:

- **Full Backup:** A full backup copies the entire database, including all data files, control files, and archived redo logs. It provides a complete snapshot of the database at a specific point in time.
- **Incremental Backup:** An incremental backup captures only the changes made since the last backup. This type of backup reduces the amount of data to be backed up and speeds up the backup process. Oracle supports both cumulative and differential incremental backups.
- **Differential Backup:** A differential backup includes all changes made since the last full backup. It is larger than incremental backups but simpler to manage.

- **Archived Redo Logs Backup:** Backup of archived redo logs, which are used to recover changes made to the database since the last backup.

2. Backup Methods:

Oracle provides several backup methods to suit different needs:

- **Cold Backup:** A cold backup is performed when the database is shut down. It ensures that all data files are consistent and can be used for recovery. This method is straightforward but requires downtime.
- **Hot Backup (Online Backup):** A hot backup is performed while the database is running. It allows users to continue working during the backup process. Oracle manages data consistency using redo logs and backup sets.
- **Incremental Backup:** Performed at regular intervals to capture only the changes since the last backup. Incremental backups are useful for minimizing backup time and storage.

8.3 Oracle Recovery Manager (RMAN)

Oracle Recovery Manager (RMAN) is a powerful tool for managing backup and recovery operations. RMAN simplifies backup and recovery tasks and provides advanced features for ensuring data protection.

1. RMAN Basics:

- **RMAN Configuration:** Configure RMAN settings to define backup locations, retention policies, and other parameters. Use the CONFIGURE command to set these parameters.
- **Creating Backups:** Use RMAN commands to create full and incremental backups. For example:

```
RMAN> BACKUP DATABASE;
RMAN> BACKUP INCREMENTAL LEVEL 1 DATABASE;
```

- **Restoring Backups:** Use RMAN to restore database files from backup. For example:

```
RMAN> RESTORE DATABASE;
RMAN> RECOVER DATABASE;
```

- **Backup Catalog:** RMAN uses a catalog to track backup metadata. You can use the RMAN catalog to view backup details and ensure backup integrity.

2. RMAN Features:

- **Backup Optimization:** RMAN optimizes backup operations to reduce storage requirements and backup time. It uses techniques like block change tracking to minimize data read.
- **Automatic Backup Management:** RMAN automatically manages backup sets, including

deleting obsolete backups based on retention policies.
- **Compression and Encryption:** RMAN supports backup compression to reduce storage requirements and encryption to protect backup data.

8.4 Data Recovery Techniques

1. Complete Recovery:

Complete recovery restores the database to the point of the last backup. It involves restoring data files and applying all available redo logs to recover changes. Example steps:

- **Restore Data Files:**

```
RMAN> RESTORE DATABASE;
```

- **Apply Redo Logs:**

```
RMAN> RECOVER DATABASE;
```

- **Open the Database:**

```
SQL> ALTER DATABASE OPEN;
```

2. Point-in-Time Recovery (PITR):

Point-in-time recovery allows you to restore the database to a specific point in time, such as before a data corruption incident. Example steps:

- **Restore Data Files:**

    ```
    RMAN> RESTORE DATABASE UNTIL TIME 'YYYY-MM-DD HH24:MI:SS';
    ```

- **Apply Redo Logs:**

    ```
    RMAN> RECOVER DATABASE;
    ```

- **Open the Database:**

    ```
    SQL> ALTER DATABASE OPEN RESETLOGS;
    ```

3. Tablespace Point-in-Time Recovery (TSPITR):

TSPITR allows recovery of specific tablespaces to a point in time, while other tablespaces remain unaffected. Example steps:

- **Prepare Tablespace for Recovery:**

```
RMAN> SET UNTIL TIME 'YYYY-MM-DD HH24:MI:SS';
RMAN> RESTORE TABLESPACE tablespace_name;
```

- **Recover Tablespace:**

```
RMAN> RECOVER TABLESPACE tablespace_name;
```

- **Open the Tablespace:**

```
SQL> ALTER TABLESPACE tablespace_name ONLINE;
```

8.5 Backup and Recovery Best Practices

1. Regular Backups:

- **Schedule Regular Backups:** Create a backup schedule that includes full, incremental, and archived redo log backups to ensure data protection and minimize data loss.
- **Monitor Backup Jobs:** Regularly monitor backup jobs and verify their completion. Use RMAN reports to review backup status and identify issues.

2. Test Backup and Recovery Procedures:

- **Regular Testing:** Periodically test backup and recovery procedures to ensure they work as expected. Perform test restores to verify the integrity of backup data.
- **Document Procedures:** Maintain documentation of backup and recovery procedures, including step-by-step instructions and contact information for support.

3. Backup Storage Management:

- **Use Reliable Storage:** Store backups on reliable storage systems with redundancy to protect against hardware failures.
- **Implement Retention Policies:** Define and enforce backup retention policies to manage backup storage efficiently and avoid accumulating obsolete backups.

4. Security of Backup Data:

- **Encrypt Backups:** Use encryption to protect backup data from unauthorized access. RMAN supports encryption for backup sets.
- **Secure Backup Locations:** Ensure backup storage locations are secure and access is restricted to authorized personnel only.

8.6 Automating Backup and Recovery

1. Backup Automation:

- **Use Oracle Enterprise Manager (OEM):** OEM provides tools for automating backup tasks and managing backup schedules. Configure backup jobs and monitor their status through the OEM interface.
- **Scripted Backups:** Use RMAN scripts to automate backup processes and schedule backups using operating system tools such as cron jobs or Windows Task Scheduler.

2. Automated Recovery:

- **Automated Failover:** Implement automated failover mechanisms using Oracle Data Guard to minimize downtime and ensure high availability.
- **Automatic Flashback:** Use Oracle's Flashback technology to quickly recover from user errors or accidental data changes without requiring traditional recovery procedures.

8.7 Summary

In this chapter, we explored Oracle Database backup and recovery techniques, including backup types and methods, RMAN features, and data recovery techniques. We also discussed best practices for backup and recovery, including regular testing, backup automation, and security measures.

Implementing a robust backup and recovery strategy ensures that your Oracle Database remains resilient and recoverable in the face of failures or disasters. By following these practices, you can safeguard your data and maintain business continuity. In the next chapter, we will delve into database administration and management, focusing on day-to-day tasks and strategies for effective database operations.

Chapter 9: Database Administration and Management

9.1 Introduction to Database Administration

Database administration involves managing and maintaining the database system to ensure its optimal performance, reliability, and security. Effective database administration includes tasks such as user management, performance monitoring, backup and recovery, and routine maintenance. This chapter will provide an overview of key database administration tasks and best practices for Oracle Database.

9.2 User and Role Management

1. User Management:

Managing database users involves creating, modifying, and deleting user accounts, as well as managing their privileges:

- **Creating Users:** Use the CREATE USER statement to create a new user account. Example:

```
CREATE USER username IDENTIFIED BY password;
```

- **Modifying Users:** Use the ALTER USER statement to change user attributes, such as password or default tablespace. Example:

```
ALTER USER username IDENTIFIED BY new_password;
```

- **Dropping Users:** Use the DROP USER statement to remove a user account. Example:

```
DROP USER username CASCADE;
```

2. Role Management:

Roles simplify the management of user privileges by grouping related permissions:

- **Creating Roles:** Use the CREATE ROLE statement to create a new role. Example:

```
CREATE ROLE role_name;
```

- **Granting Privileges to Roles:** Use the GRANT statement to assign privileges to a role. Example:

```
GRANT SELECT, INSERT ON table_name TO role_name;
```

- **Assigning Roles to Users:** Use the GRANT statement to assign roles to users. Example:

```
GRANT role_name TO username;
```

- **Revoking Roles:** Use the REVOKE statement to remove roles from users. Example:

```
REVOKE role_name FROM username;
```

9.3 Performance Monitoring and Tuning

1. Monitoring Tools:

Monitoring tools help track database performance and identify potential issues:

- **Oracle Enterprise Manager (OEM):** Provides a comprehensive interface for monitoring database performance, generating alerts, and viewing performance metrics.
- **Automatic Workload Repository (AWR):** Collects performance statistics and generates reports to help analyze database performance over time.
- **Oracle SQL Developer:** Offers performance monitoring and tuning features, including execution plans and query analysis.

2. Performance Tuning:

Performance tuning involves optimizing database performance by adjusting configuration settings and queries:

- **Analyzing Execution Plans:** Use the EXPLAIN PLAN statement to view the execution plan of a query and identify areas for optimization. Example:

```
EXPLAIN PLAN FOR SELECT * FROM table_name;
```

- **Index Optimization:** Ensure that indexes are created on frequently queried columns and regularly maintained to enhance query performance.
- **SQL Tuning:** Optimize SQL queries by rewriting them for efficiency, using appropriate indexing, and avoiding unnecessary computations.

9.4 Database Maintenance Tasks

Routine maintenance tasks ensure the database operates smoothly and efficiently:

1. Regular Backups:

- **Schedule Backups:** Implement a backup schedule that includes full, incremental, and archived redo log backups to ensure data protection.
- **Monitor Backup Jobs:** Regularly check the status of backup jobs and verify their completion.

2. Updating Statistics:

- **Gather Statistics:** Use the DBMS_STATS package to gather and update database statistics for optimal query performance. Example:

```
EXEC DBMS_STATS.GATHER_DATABASE_STATS;
```

3. Rebuilding Indexes:

- **Rebuild Indexes:** Rebuild fragmented indexes to improve query performance and reduce storage overhead. Example:

```
ALTER INDEX index_name REBUILD;
```

4. Managing Tablespaces:

- **Monitor Tablespace Usage:** Regularly check tablespace usage to ensure adequate space is available. Use the DBA_DATA_FILES and DBA_FREE_SPACE views for monitoring.
- **Extend Tablespaces:** Add data files or increase the size of existing data files to accommodate growing data requirements. Example:

```
ALTER DATABASE DATAFILE 'file_name' RESIZE 100M;
```

9.5 Backup and Recovery

Effective backup and recovery practices are essential for protecting data and ensuring business continuity:

1. Backup Strategies:

- **Implement Backup Policies:** Define and enforce backup policies that specify backup frequency, retention, and storage locations.
- **Automate Backups:** Use Oracle's RMAN tool to automate backup processes and schedule regular backups.

2. Recovery Procedures:

- **Perform Test Restores:** Regularly test backup and recovery procedures to verify their effectiveness and ensure you can recover data when needed.
- **Develop a Recovery Plan:** Create a detailed recovery plan that outlines steps for restoring the database in case of failure or data loss.

9.6 Security Management

Ensuring database security is a critical aspect of database administration:

1. Implement Security Policies:

- **Define Access Controls:** Establish access controls to restrict user permissions based on their roles and responsibilities.

- **Use Encryption:** Implement data encryption to protect sensitive data both at rest and in transit.

2. Monitor Security:

- **Audit Database Activity:** Use Oracle's auditing features to track and monitor database activities, including login attempts and changes to data.
- **Respond to Security Incidents:** Develop procedures for responding to and mitigating security incidents, including data breaches or unauthorized access.

9.7 Disaster Recovery Planning

Preparing for disaster scenarios ensures that the database can be quickly restored and operational:

1. Develop a Disaster Recovery Plan:

- **Plan for Various Scenarios:** Create a plan that covers different types of disasters, such as hardware failures, data corruption, or natural disasters.
- **Define Recovery Objectives:** Establish recovery time objectives (RTO) and recovery point objectives (RPO) to guide your recovery efforts.

2. Test Disaster Recovery:

- **Conduct Regular Drills:** Perform disaster recovery drills to test your recovery procedures and ensure that your team is prepared for emergencies.
- **Review and Update the Plan:** Regularly review and update the disaster recovery plan to address changes

in your database environment and business requirements.

9.8 Database Upgrades and Patching

Keeping your database environment up-to-date with the latest patches and versions is essential for maintaining security and performance:

1. Apply Patches:

- **Install Critical Patches:** Regularly apply Oracle's Critical Patch Updates (CPUs) to address security vulnerabilities and bugs.
- **Test Patches:** Before applying patches to production environments, test them in a development or staging environment to ensure compatibility and stability.

2. Upgrade Database Versions:

- **Plan Upgrades:** Plan and execute database upgrades to take advantage of new features and improvements in newer versions of Oracle Database.
- **Perform Compatibility Checks:** Check for compatibility issues and test applications to ensure they work with the upgraded database version.

9.9 Summary

In this chapter, we explored key aspects of database administration and management, including user and role management, performance monitoring and tuning, routine maintenance tasks, backup and recovery, security management, disaster recovery planning, and database upgrades and patching.

Effective database administration ensures that your Oracle Database remains performant, secure, and reliable. By following best practices and implementing robust management strategies, you can maintain a well-functioning database environment that supports your organization's needs. In the next chapter, we will discuss advanced Oracle Database features and capabilities, including partitioning, parallel processing, and advanced analytics.

Chapter 10: Advanced Oracle Database Features

10.1 Introduction to Advanced Features

Oracle Database offers a rich set of advanced features that enhance performance, scalability, and data management capabilities. These features address complex data processing needs and support large-scale and mission-critical applications. This chapter explores several advanced Oracle Database features, including partitioning, parallel processing, advanced analytics, and more.

10.2 Partitioning

Partitioning divides large tables and indexes into smaller, more manageable pieces while maintaining the logical structure of the database. Partitioning improves performance, manageability, and availability.

1. Types of Partitioning:

- **Range Partitioning:** Divides data based on a range of values, such as dates. Each partition holds a specific range of values. Example:

```
CREATE TABLE sales (
    sale_date DATE,
    amount NUMBER
)
PARTITION BY RANGE (sale_date) (
    PARTITION p1 VALUES LESS THAN
(TO_DATE('2024-01-01', 'YYYY-MM-DD')),
    PARTITION p2 VALUES LESS THAN
(TO_DATE('2025-01-01', 'YYYY-MM-DD'))
);
```

- **List Partitioning:** Divides data based on discrete values or lists of values. Each partition holds specific values. Example:

```
CREATE TABLE customer_orders (
    customer_id NUMBER,
    order_type VARCHAR2(10)
)
PARTITION BY LIST (order_type) (
    PARTITION p1 VALUES ('Online'),
    PARTITION p2 VALUES ('In-Store')
);
```

- **Hash Partitioning:** Distributes data across partitions based on a hash function. This method balances data distribution and is useful for evenly spreading large datasets. Example:

```
CREATE TABLE employee (
   employee_id NUMBER,
   department_id NUMBER
)
PARTITION BY HASH (department_id) PARTITIONS 4;
```

- **Composite Partitioning:** Combines multiple partitioning methods. For example, you can use range-hash partitioning to partition data by range first and then by hash within each range partition.

2. Benefits of Partitioning:

- **Improved Query Performance:** Queries can be optimized by scanning only relevant partitions, reducing I/O and processing time.
- **Enhanced Manageability:** Backup, recovery, and maintenance operations can be performed on individual partitions, reducing downtime and complexity.
- **Better Data Organization:** Partitioning helps manage large tables and indexes by logically grouping related data.

10.3 Parallel Processing

Parallel processing allows Oracle Database to perform multiple operations simultaneously, improving performance for large-scale queries and data manipulation tasks.

1. Parallel Query:

Parallel query execution divides a query into smaller tasks that run concurrently across multiple processors. This approach accelerates query processing for large datasets. Example:

- **Enabling Parallel Query:**

```
ALTER TABLE sales PARALLEL (DEGREE 4);
```

- **Executing a Parallel Query:**

```
SELECT /*+ PARALLEL(sales, 4) */ * FROM sales;
```

2. Parallel DML:

Parallel Data Manipulation Language (DML) allows concurrent execution of DML operations, such as INSERT, UPDATE, and DELETE, across multiple processors. This enhances the efficiency of large data loads and updates.

- **Enabling Parallel DML:**

```
ALTER SESSION ENABLE PARALLEL DML;
```

- **Executing a Parallel DML Operation:**

```
INSERT /*+ PARALLEL(sales, 4) */ INTO sales_backup
SELECT * FROM sales;
```

3. Parallel Index Creation:

Parallel index creation speeds up the creation of indexes by distributing the work across multiple processors.

- **Creating a Parallel Index:**

```
CREATE INDEX idx_sales ON sales(amount)
PARALLEL (DEGREE 4);
```

10.4 Advanced Analytics

Oracle Database includes powerful analytics capabilities for advanced data analysis and business intelligence.

1. Oracle OLAP:

Oracle OLAP (Online Analytical Processing) provides multidimensional analysis capabilities, allowing users to perform complex queries and analyses on large datasets.

- **Creating an OLAP Cube:**

```
CREATE CUBE sales_cube
DIMENSION BY (product_category, region, time)
MEASURE sales_amount;
```

- **Querying an OLAP Cube:**

```
SELECT * FROM sales_cube
WHERE region = 'North America';
```

2. Oracle Data Mining:

Oracle Data Mining offers machine learning algorithms and data mining techniques for discovering patterns and making predictions from data.

- **Building a Classification Model:**

```
BEGIN
  DBMS_DATA_MINING.CREATE_MODEL(
    model_name => 'model_classify',
    algorithm =>
DBMS_DATA_MINING.CLASSIFICATION,
    data_table_name => 'customer_data',
    target_column => 'customer_segment'
  );
END;
```

- **Scoring Data:**

```
SELECT customer_id,
DBMS_DATA_MINING.PREDICT('model_classify',
customer_data)
FROM customer_data;
```

3. Oracle Spatial and Graph:

Oracle Spatial and Graph provide capabilities for managing spatial data, performing geographic analyses, and working with graph data structures.

- **Creating a Spatial Index:**

```
CREATE INDEX idx_location ON locations(location)
INDEXTYPE IS MDSYS.SPATIAL_INDEX;
```

- **Querying Spatial Data:**

```
SELECT * FROM locations
WHERE SDO_NN(location, SDO_GEOMETRY(2001,
NULL, SDO_POINT_TYPE(1, 1, NULL), NULL, NULL),
'all') = 'TRUE';
```

4. Oracle Text:

Oracle Text provides full-text search capabilities, allowing users to search and index textual data efficiently.

- **Creating a Text Index:**

```
CREATE INDEX idx_text ON documents(text_column)
INDEXTYPE IS CTXSYS.CONTEXT;
```

- **Performing a Text Search:**

```
SELECT * FROM documents
WHERE CONTAINS(text_column, 'search term') > 0;
```

10.5 Flashback Technology

Oracle Flashback technology allows you to view and restore past states of data, making it easier to recover from accidental data changes or deletions.

1. Flashback Query:

Flashback Query enables you to retrieve data as it existed at a specific point in time.

- **Querying Historical Data:**

```
SELECT * FROM sales
AS OF TIMESTAMP (SYSTIMESTAMP - INTERVAL '1' HOUR);
```

2. Flashback Table:

Flashback Table restores an entire table to its state at a previous point in time.

- **Restoring a Table:**

```
FLASHBACK TABLE sales TO TIMESTAMP
(SYSTIMESTAMP - INTERVAL '1' DAY);
```

3. Flashback Drop:

Flashback Drop allows you to recover dropped tables from the recycle bin.

- **Recovering a Dropped Table:**

```
FLASHBACK TABLE dropped_table TO BEFORE DROP;
```

10.6 Materialized Views

Materialized views are database objects that store the result of a query and are used to improve performance by pre-computing and storing complex query results.

1. Creating a Materialized View:

- **Creating a Simple Materialized View:**

```
CREATE MATERIALIZED VIEW sales_summary
AS SELECT product_category, SUM(amount) AS
total_sales
FROM sales
GROUP BY product_category;
```

- **Refreshing a Materialized View:**

```
BEGIN
  DBMS_MVIEW.REFRESH('sales_summary');
END;
```

2. Using Materialized View Logs:

Materialized view logs capture changes to the base tables and enable fast refreshes of materialized views.

- **Creating a Materialized View Log:**

```
CREATE MATERIALIZED VIEW LOG ON sales
WITH ROWID, SEQUENCE (product_category,
amount);
```

10.7 Summary

In this chapter, we explored advanced Oracle Database features that enhance performance, scalability, and data management. We covered partitioning, parallel processing, advanced analytics, Flashback technology, materialized views, and more. These features provide powerful tools for optimizing database operations and addressing complex data processing needs.

By leveraging these advanced capabilities, you can improve the efficiency and effectiveness of your Oracle Database environment. In the next chapter, we will delve into best practices for database design and modeling, focusing on designing scalable and efficient database schemas.

Chapter 11: Best Practices for Database Design and Modeling

11.1 Introduction to Database Design

Effective database design is crucial for creating scalable, efficient, and maintainable database systems. A well-designed database schema supports robust performance, simplifies data management, and ensures data integrity. This chapter covers best practices for database design and modeling, including normalization, schema design, and entity-relationship modeling.

11.2 Normalization

Normalization is the process of organizing data within a database to reduce redundancy and improve data integrity. The goal is to design a schema that minimizes data duplication and ensures consistency.

1. Normal Forms:

Normalization involves applying a series of normal forms, each with specific criteria for organizing data:

- **First Normal Form (1NF):** Ensures that each column contains atomic (indivisible) values and that each record is unique.

- Example:

```
CREATE TABLE orders (
   order_id NUMBER PRIMARY KEY,
   customer_id NUMBER,
   order_date DATE,
   item_name VARCHAR2(50),
   item_quantity NUMBER
);
```

- **Second Normal Form (2NF):** Achieved when a table is in 1NF and all non-key attributes are fully functionally dependent on the primary key. Example:

```
CREATE TABLE orders (
   order_id NUMBER PRIMARY KEY,
   customer_id NUMBER,
   order_date DATE
);
```

```
CREATE TABLE order_items (
   order_id NUMBER,
   item_name VARCHAR2(50),
   item_quantity NUMBER,
   PRIMARY KEY (order_id, item_name),
   FOREIGN KEY (order_id) REFERENCES orders(order_id)
);
```

- **Third Normal Form (3NF):** Achieved when a table is in 2NF and all attributes are directly dependent on the primary key, with no transitive dependencies. Example:

```
CREATE TABLE customers (
    customer_id NUMBER PRIMARY KEY,
    customer_name VARCHAR2(100),
    customer_address VARCHAR2(255)
);
```

2. De-Normalization:

In some cases, de-normalization is used to improve performance by introducing redundancy for optimization purposes. This technique involves combining tables to reduce the need for complex joins.

- **Example of De-Normalization:**

```
CREATE TABLE order_summary (
    order_id NUMBER PRIMARY KEY,
    customer_name VARCHAR2(100),
    order_date DATE,
    item_name VARCHAR2(50),
    item_quantity NUMBER
);
```

11.3 Schema Design

Schema design involves structuring the database schema to support application requirements and ensure data integrity. Key aspects of schema design include defining tables, columns, relationships, and constraints.

1. Table Design:

- **Define Tables:** Create tables to represent entities, with columns corresponding to attributes. Choose appropriate data types and sizes for each column.

```
CREATE TABLE employees (
    employee_id NUMBER PRIMARY KEY,
    first_name VARCHAR2(50),
    last_name VARCHAR2(50),
    hire_date DATE,
    salary NUMBER
);
```

- **Use Constraints:** Apply constraints to enforce data integrity and business rules. Common constraints include PRIMARY KEY, FOREIGN KEY, UNIQUE, and CHECK constraints.

```
ALTER TABLE employees
ADD CONSTRAINT salary_check CHECK (salary > 0);
```

2. Relationships:

- **Define Relationships:** Use foreign keys to establish relationships between tables. Ensure referential integrity by defining appropriate foreign key constraints.

```sql
CREATE TABLE departments (
    department_id NUMBER PRIMARY KEY,
    department_name VARCHAR2(50)
);

ALTER TABLE employees
ADD CONSTRAINT fk_department
FOREIGN KEY (department_id) REFERENCES departments(department_id);
```

- **Implement Many-to-Many Relationships:** Use junction tables to manage many-to-many relationships between entities.

```sql
CREATE TABLE student_courses (
    student_id NUMBER,
    course_id NUMBER,
    PRIMARY KEY (student_id, course_id),
    FOREIGN KEY (student_id) REFERENCES students(student_id),
    FOREIGN KEY (course_id) REFERENCES courses(course_id)
);
```

11.4 Entity-Relationship (ER) Modeling

Entity-Relationship (ER) modeling is a technique for visually representing database schema and relationships between entities. ER diagrams help design and communicate the structure of the database.

1. Creating ER Diagrams:

- **Identify Entities:** Identify the entities to be modeled (e.g., customers, orders, products).
- **Define Attributes:** Define the attributes for each entity (e.g., customer name, order date).
- **Establish Relationships:** Define relationships between entities (e.g., customers place orders).
- **Example ER Diagram:**

```
[Customer] --< Places >-- [Order] --< Contains >-- [Product]
```

2. ER Diagram Symbols:

- **Entities:** Represented by rectangles, with attributes listed inside.
- **Relationships:** Represented by diamonds, connecting entities.
- **Attributes:** Represented by ovals, connected to entities.
- **Primary Keys:** Underlined attributes that uniquely identify each record.

11.5 Designing for Performance

Designing a database schema with performance in mind ensures efficient query execution and data management.

1. Indexing:

- **Create Indexes:** Use indexes to speed up data retrieval operations. Choose columns frequently used in search conditions and joins for indexing.

```
CREATE INDEX idx_employee_salary ON employees(salary);
```

- **Monitor Index Usage:** Regularly review index usage and performance to ensure indexes are effective and not causing overhead.

2. Partitioning:

- **Apply Partitioning:** Use partitioning to manage large tables and improve query performance by dividing data into smaller, manageable pieces.

```sql
CREATE TABLE sales (
    sale_date DATE,
    amount NUMBER
)
PARTITION BY RANGE (sale_date) (
    PARTITION p1 VALUES LESS THAN
(TO_DATE('2024-01-01', 'YYYY-MM-DD')),
    PARTITION p2 VALUES LESS THAN
(TO_DATE('2025-01-01', 'YYYY-MM-DD'))
);
```

3. Data Archiving:

- **Implement Archiving Strategies:** Archive historical or infrequently accessed data to improve the performance of active data processing.

```sql
CREATE TABLE sales_archive AS
SELECT * FROM sales
WHERE sale_date < SYSDATE - INTERVAL '1' YEAR;
```

11.6 Data Integrity and Validation

Ensuring data integrity and validation is essential for maintaining accurate and reliable data in the database.

1. **Implement Constraints:**

    - **Use Constraints:** Apply constraints to enforce rules and ensure data accuracy. Common constraints include UNIQUE, CHECK, and FOREIGN KEY.

    ```
    ALTER TABLE orders
    ADD CONSTRAINT fk_customer
    FOREIGN KEY (customer_id) REFERENCES
    customers(customer_id);
    ```

    - **Validate Data:** Use CHECK constraints to enforce domain constraints and ensure data values meet specific criteria.

    ```
    ALTER TABLE employees
    ADD CONSTRAINT salary_check CHECK (salary > 0);
    ```

2. **Data Quality Checks:**

    - **Regular Audits:** Perform regular data quality audits to identify and rectify inconsistencies or inaccuracies.
    - **Automated Validation:** Implement automated validation scripts to check data integrity and consistency.

11.7 Documentation and Communication

Effective documentation and communication are critical for ensuring that database design and modeling efforts align with business requirements and stakeholder expectations.

1. Document Design Decisions:

- **Schema Documentation:** Document the database schema, including table structures, relationships, and constraints.
- **Design Rationale:** Provide explanations for design decisions, including normalization choices and indexing strategies.

2. Communicate with Stakeholders:

- **Engage Stakeholders:** Collaborate with business stakeholders to understand requirements and ensure the design meets their needs.
- **Present ER Diagrams:** Use ER diagrams to visually communicate the database structure and relationships to non-technical stakeholders.

11.8 Summary

In this chapter, we covered best practices for database design and modeling, including normalization, schema design, ER modeling, performance optimization, and data integrity. A well-designed database schema enhances data management, improves performance, and supports business requirements effectively.

By following these best practices, you can create a robust and efficient database system that meets your organization's needs. In the next chapter, we will explore database security, focusing on securing your Oracle Database environment against unauthorized access and vulnerabilities.

Chapter 12: Database Security

12.1 Introduction to Database Security

Database security is essential for protecting sensitive data, ensuring compliance with regulations, and maintaining the integrity and availability of the database system. This chapter explores key aspects of database security, including user access control, data encryption, auditing, and best practices for securing your Oracle Database environment.

12.2 User Access Control

User access control involves managing who can access the database and what actions they can perform. Effective user access control minimizes the risk of unauthorized access and data breaches.

1. User Accounts and Roles:

- **Creating User Accounts:** Use the CREATE USER statement to create new database users. Example:

```
CREATE USER username IDENTIFIED BY password;
```

- **Granting Roles and Privileges:** Assign roles and privileges to users to control their access. Use the GRANT statement to provide specific privileges. Example:

```
GRANT SELECT, INSERT ON table_name TO
username;
```

- **Revoking Roles and Privileges:** Remove roles and privileges when they are no longer needed. Example:

```
REVOKE SELECT ON table_name FROM username;
```

2. Role-Based Access Control (RBAC):

- **Creating Roles:** Define roles to group related privileges. Example:

```
CREATE ROLE analyst;
```

- **Assigning Roles to Users:** Grant roles to users to simplify privilege management. Example:

```
GRANT analyst TO username;
```

- **Role Hierarchies:** Use role hierarchies to organize roles and manage permissions more efficiently.

3. Privilege Management:

- **Fine-Grained Privileges:** Use fine-grained access control to manage permissions at a more granular level. Example:

```
CREATE VIEW sensitive_data_view AS
SELECT sensitive_column FROM sensitive_table
WHERE user_role = SESSION_USER;
```

- **Data Masking:** Implement data masking to obfuscate sensitive data in non-production environments.

12.3 Data Encryption

Data encryption protects sensitive information by converting it into an unreadable format, which can only be decrypted by authorized users.

1. Transparent Data Encryption (TDE):

- **Enabling TDE:** TDE encrypts data at rest, including data files, redo logs, and backups. Example:

```
ALTER SYSTEM SET ENCRYPTION KEY IDENTIFIED BY "key_password";
```

- **Encrypting Tablespaces:** Create encrypted tablespaces to protect sensitive data.

```
CREATE TABLESPACE encrypted_ts
ENCRYPTION USING 'AES256'
DATAFILE 'encrypted_ts.dbf' SIZE 100M;
```

2. Column-Level Encryption:

- **Encrypting Columns:** Use column-level encryption to encrypt specific columns within a table.

```
CREATE TABLE employees (
    employee_id NUMBER PRIMARY KEY,
    name VARCHAR2(50),
    ssn VARCHAR2(20) ENCRYPT
);
```

3. Data Encryption in Transit:

- **SSL/TLS Encryption:** Use SSL/TLS to encrypt data transmitted between clients and the database server. Configure Oracle Net Services to support SSL/TLS connections.

```
SQLNET.ENCRYPTION_TYPES_SERVER = (TLS)
SQLNET.ENCRYPTION_SERVER = required
```

12.4 Auditing and Monitoring

Auditing and monitoring help detect and respond to unauthorized access, data breaches, and other security incidents.

1. Oracle Auditing:

- **Standard Auditing:** Use standard auditing to track database activities and generate audit logs. Configure auditing for specific actions, such as login attempts or data modifications.

```
AUDIT SELECT ON employees BY ACCESS;
```

- **Fine-Grained Auditing (FGA):** Implement fine-grained auditing to capture detailed audit information based on user roles and data access patterns.

```
BEGIN
  DBMS_FGA.ADD_POLICY(
    object_schema => 'HR',
    object_name => 'EMPLOYEES',
    policy_name => 'audit_policy',
    audit_condition => 'SALARY > 100000',
    audit_column => 'SALARY'
  );
END;
```

2. Monitoring Tools:

- **Oracle Enterprise Manager (OEM):** Use OEM to monitor database performance, track security events, and generate alerts.
- **Oracle Audit Vault and Database Firewall:** Implement Oracle Audit Vault and Database Firewall to consolidate audit data, monitor for suspicious activities, and enforce security policies.

3. Reviewing Audit Logs:

- **Regular Reviews:** Regularly review audit logs to detect anomalies and unauthorized activities. Analyze logs to identify potential security threats and take corrective actions.

12.5 Database Hardening

Database hardening involves configuring the database system to reduce vulnerabilities and enhance security.

1. Configuration Best Practices:

- **Disable Unused Features:** Turn off features and services that are not in use to minimize the attack surface.
- **Apply Security Patches:** Regularly apply security patches and updates to address known vulnerabilities.

```
opatch apply <patch_number>
```

- **Secure Configuration Settings:** Review and configure database settings to enhance security, such as disabling remote login and restricting access to sensitive features.

2. Network Security:

- **Firewall Rules:** Configure firewall rules to restrict access to the database server from unauthorized IP addresses.
- **Network Segmentation:** Use network segmentation to isolate database servers from other parts of the network.

3. Secure Backup and Recovery:

- **Encrypt Backups:** Ensure that backups are encrypted to protect data in case of backup media theft or loss.

```
RMAN> CONFIGURE ENCRYPTION FOR DATABASE ON;
```

- **Implement Backup Policies:** Define and enforce backup policies to ensure regular and secure backup operations.

12.6 Compliance and Regulatory Requirements

Compliance with regulations and industry standards is crucial for maintaining database security and protecting sensitive data.

1. **Regulatory Frameworks:**

    - **General Data Protection Regulation (GDPR):** Ensure compliance with GDPR requirements for data protection and privacy.
    - **Health Insurance Portability and Accountability Act (HIPAA):** Implement measures to protect health information and ensure compliance with HIPAA regulations.
    - **Payment Card Industry Data Security Standard (PCI-DSS):** Follow PCI-DSS guidelines for securing payment card information.

2. **Documentation and Reporting:**

    - **Maintain Documentation:** Keep detailed records of security policies, procedures, and compliance efforts.
    - **Generate Reports:** Create reports to demonstrate compliance with regulatory requirements and audit findings.

12.7 Incident Response and Recovery

Preparing for and responding to security incidents is essential for minimizing the impact of data breaches and other security events.

1. **Incident Response Plan:**

    - **Develop a Plan:** Create a detailed incident response plan that outlines procedures for detecting, responding to, and recovering from security incidents.

- **Define Roles and Responsibilities:** Assign roles and responsibilities to team members involved in incident response and recovery efforts.

2. Response Procedures:

- **Contain and Mitigate:** Take immediate action to contain and mitigate the impact of the security incident.
- **Investigate and Analyze:** Conduct a thorough investigation to understand the cause of the incident and assess its impact.
- **Recover and Restore:** Restore normal operations and implement measures to prevent similar incidents in the future.

3. Post-Incident Review:

- **Conduct a Review:** Perform a post-incident review to evaluate the effectiveness of the response and identify areas for improvement.
- **Update Procedures:** Update incident response procedures and security measures based on lessons learned from the incident.

12.8 Summary

In this chapter, we explored key aspects of database security, including user access control, data encryption, auditing and monitoring, database hardening, compliance with regulatory requirements, and incident response. Implementing robust security measures and best practices helps protect your

Oracle Database environment from unauthorized access, data breaches, and other security threats.

By following these guidelines, you can ensure the security and integrity of your database system while meeting regulatory requirements and safeguarding sensitive data. In the next chapter, we will discuss database migration and integration strategies, focusing on moving data between systems and integrating Oracle Database with other technologies.

Chapter 13: Database Migration and Integration

13.1 Introduction to Database Migration and Integration

Database migration and integration are crucial for modernizing database systems, improving performance, and ensuring compatibility with other technologies. This chapter explores strategies and best practices for migrating databases between systems and integrating Oracle Database with other technologies.

13.2 Database Migration Strategies

Database migration involves moving data and applications from one database system to another. This process can be complex and requires careful planning to minimize downtime and ensure data integrity.

1. Types of Database Migration:

- **Homogeneous Migration:** Moving data between identical database systems (e.g., Oracle to Oracle). Typically simpler as the source and target systems use the same database engine.
- **Heterogeneous Migration:** Moving data between different database systems (e.g., Oracle to SQL Server). Requires more complex transformations and mapping.

2. Migration Planning:

- **Assess the Source Database:** Analyze the source database for its structure, data types, and

relationships. Identify any dependencies and customizations.
- **Define Migration Objectives:** Set clear objectives for the migration, such as improving performance, upgrading to a newer version, or consolidating databases.
- **Choose a Migration Tool:** Select a migration tool based on your requirements. Common tools include Oracle Data Pump, Oracle GoldenGate, and third-party migration solutions.

3. Migration Steps:

- **Schema Migration:** Migrate database schema (tables, indexes, constraints) using tools like Oracle SQL Developer or schema migration utilities.

```
-- Example of exporting schema
expdp user/password DIRECTORY=dp_dir
DUMPFILE=schema.dmp SCHEMAS=schema_name;
```

- **Data Migration:** Transfer data from the source database to the target database. Use tools like Oracle Data Pump, SQL*Loader, or data migration utilities provided by the target database.

```
-- Example of importing data
impdp user/password DIRECTORY=dp_dir
DUMPFILE=data.dmp LOGFILE=import.log;
```

- **Application Migration:** Update application configurations and code to work with the new database system. Ensure compatibility with the migrated schema and data.
- **Testing and Validation:** Perform thorough testing to ensure that the migrated database functions as expected. Validate data integrity, application performance, and query results.
- **Go-Live and Cutover:** Plan and execute the go-live process. Minimize downtime and ensure a smooth transition to the new database system.

4. Post-Migration Tasks:

- **Monitor Performance:** Monitor the performance of the new database system and address any issues that arise.
- **Optimize and Tune:** Optimize database performance by tuning queries, indexes, and configurations based on the new environment.
- **Backup and Documentation:** Create backups of the new database and document the migration process for future reference.

13.3 Database Integration Strategies

Database integration involves connecting Oracle Database with other systems and technologies to enable seamless data exchange and interoperability.

1. **Integration with Other Databases:**

    - **Database Links:** Use database links to enable communication between Oracle databases and access remote data.

    ```
    CREATE DATABASE LINK remote_db
    CONNECT TO remote_user IDENTIFIED BY remote_password
    USING 'remote_tns_service';
    ```

    - **Data Integration Tools:** Use data integration tools like Oracle Data Integrator (ODI) to move and synchronize data between different databases.

2. **Integration with Applications:**

    - **Application Programming Interfaces (APIs):** Use APIs to integrate Oracle Database with applications. Oracle provides APIs for various programming languages and frameworks.

    ```
    // Example of connecting to Oracle Database using JDBC
    Connection conn = DriverManager.getConnection("jdbc:oracle:thin:@localhost:1521:orcl", "user", "password");
    ```

- **Middleware Solutions:** Use middleware solutions like Oracle Fusion Middleware to connect Oracle Database with enterprise applications and services.

3. Integration with Cloud Services:

- **Oracle Cloud Infrastructure (OCI):** Integrate Oracle Database with Oracle Cloud services for scalability, high availability, and advanced features.

  ```
  -- Example of creating an Oracle Cloud Autonomous Database instance
  CREATE DATABASE INSTANCE my_autonomous_db;
  ```

- **Third-Party Cloud Services:** Use connectors and integration tools to connect Oracle Database with third-party cloud services, such as AWS or Microsoft Azure.

4. Data Synchronization:

- **Oracle GoldenGate:** Use Oracle GoldenGate for real-time data replication and synchronization between databases.

  ```
  -- Example of configuring Oracle GoldenGate replication
  ADD EXTRACT ext1, TRANLOG, BEGIN NOW;
  ```

- **Materialized Views:** Use materialized views to create and maintain snapshots of data for reporting and integration purposes.

```
CREATE MATERIALIZED VIEW sales_summary
AS SELECT product_id, SUM(sales_amount) AS total_sales
FROM sales
GROUP BY product_id;
```

13.4 Best Practices for Migration and Integration

1. Plan and Test:

- **Create a Migration Plan:** Develop a detailed migration plan that outlines the steps, timelines, and resources required.
- **Perform Thorough Testing:** Test the migration and integration processes in a staging environment before deploying to production.

2. Minimize Downtime:

- **Schedule During Off-Peak Hours:** Perform migration and integration tasks during off-peak hours to minimize impact on users.
- **Use Zero-Downtime Techniques:** Employ techniques like rolling upgrades and online migrations to minimize downtime.

3. Ensure Data Integrity:

- **Verify Data Consistency:** Check for data consistency and integrity throughout the migration and integration processes.
- **Handle Data Transformations:** Ensure that data transformations and mappings are accurate and preserve data quality.

4. Monitor and Optimize:

- **Monitor Performance:** Continuously monitor the performance of the migrated and integrated systems to identify and address issues.
- **Optimize Configurations:** Optimize database and application configurations to improve performance and reliability.

5. Document and Train:

- **Document Processes:** Document the migration and integration processes, configurations, and any customizations.
- **Provide Training:** Train users and administrators on the new system and any changes resulting from migration or integration.

13.5 Summary

In this chapter, we explored database migration and integration strategies, including migration planning, execution, and post-migration tasks, as well as integration with other databases, applications, and cloud services. We also covered best practices for ensuring a smooth and successful migration and integration process.

By following these guidelines, you can effectively migrate and integrate Oracle Database with other systems and technologies, enhancing your database environment and meeting your organization's needs. In the next chapter, we will discuss performance tuning and optimization strategies for Oracle Database, focusing on improving query performance, resource utilization, and overall system efficiency.

Chapter 14: Performance Tuning and Optimization

14.1 Introduction to Performance Tuning

Performance tuning is the process of improving the efficiency and effectiveness of a database system to ensure optimal performance and resource utilization. In Oracle Database, performance tuning involves various techniques and strategies to enhance query performance, manage system resources, and address bottlenecks. This chapter explores key aspects of performance tuning and optimization for Oracle Database.

14.2 Understanding Performance Metrics

Before diving into tuning, it's essential to understand the metrics and tools used to measure database performance.

1. Key Performance Metrics:

- **Response Time:** The time taken to execute a query or perform a transaction. Lower response times indicate better performance.
- **Throughput:** The number of transactions or queries processed in a given period. Higher throughput indicates better performance.
- **Resource Utilization:** The usage of system resources such as CPU, memory, and disk I/O. Efficient resource utilization is crucial for optimal performance.
- **Wait Events:** Events where the database waits for resources or conditions to proceed. Analyzing wait events helps identify bottlenecks.

2. Performance Monitoring Tools:

- **Oracle Enterprise Manager (OEM):** Provides a comprehensive interface for monitoring database performance, including real-time metrics and historical data.
- **Automatic Workload Repository (AWR):** Collects and stores performance data, including wait events, SQL execution statistics, and system resources.
- **Statspack:** An older performance monitoring tool similar to AWR, used for capturing and analyzing performance metrics.

14.3 Query Optimization

Query optimization focuses on improving the performance of SQL queries. Effective optimization can significantly reduce query execution times and resource consumption.

1. Analyzing Query Execution Plans:

- **Explain Plan:** Use the EXPLAIN PLAN statement to generate an execution plan for a SQL query. The execution plan shows how the database will execute the query.

```
EXPLAIN PLAN FOR
SELECT * FROM employees WHERE department_id = 10;

SELECT * FROM TABLE(DBMS_XPLAN.DISPLAY);
```

- **Cost-Based Optimization:** Oracle's cost-based optimizer evaluates different execution plans and selects the most efficient one based on cost estimates.

2. Indexing:

- **Creating Indexes:** Create indexes to improve query performance, especially for columns used in search conditions and joins.

```
CREATE INDEX idx_employee_dept ON
employees(department_id);
```

- **Index Maintenance:** Regularly monitor and rebuild indexes to ensure they remain effective. Use ALTER INDEX ... REBUILD to rebuild fragmented indexes.

3. SQL Tuning:

- **Avoid Full Table Scans:** Use indexes and optimize queries to avoid full table scans, which can be resource-intensive.
- **Optimize Joins:** Use appropriate join types (e.g., inner join, outer join) and ensure that join conditions are efficient.

```
SELECT e.employee_id, e.name, d.department_name
FROM employees e
```

```
JOIN departments d ON e.department_id =
d.department_id;
```

- **Use Bind Variables:** Use bind variables to improve query performance and reduce parsing overhead.

```
SELECT * FROM employees WHERE department_id =
:dept_id;
```

14.4 Resource Management

Effective resource management ensures that database resources such as CPU, memory, and disk I/O are used efficiently.

1. Managing CPU Resources:

- **Resource Manager:** Use Oracle Resource Manager to allocate CPU resources among different database workloads and users.

```
BEGIN
  DBMS_RESOURCE_MANAGER.CREATE_PLAN(
    PLAN => 'cpu_plan',
    COMMENTS => 'CPU resource management plan'
  );
END;
```

- **Optimize Queries:** Ensure that queries and transactions are optimized to minimize CPU usage.

2. Managing Memory:

- **Automatic Memory Management (AMM):** Use AMM to dynamically allocate and manage memory resources for the database.

```
ALTER SYSTEM SET MEMORY_TARGET = 2G;
```

- **PGA and SGA Tuning:** Adjust Program Global Area (PGA) and System Global Area (SGA) settings based on workload requirements.

```
ALTER SYSTEM SET PGA_AGGREGATE_TARGET = 1G;
ALTER SYSTEM SET SGA_TARGET = 1.5G;
```

3. Managing Disk I/O:

- **Optimize I/O Operations:** Use techniques like partitioning and striping to improve disk I/O performance.
- **Monitor I/O Performance:** Use Oracle's performance views and tools to monitor disk I/O and identify potential issues.

```
SELECT * FROM v$filestat;
```

14.5 Database Configuration and Tuning

Database configuration and tuning involve adjusting database settings to optimize performance and ensure efficient operation.

1. Initialization Parameters:

- **Tune Parameters:** Adjust initialization parameters based on workload requirements and performance goals. Common parameters include DB_CACHE_SIZE, LOG_BUFFER, and UNDO_TABLESPACE.

```
ALTER SYSTEM SET DB_CACHE_SIZE = 512M;
ALTER SYSTEM SET LOG_BUFFER = 8M;
```

- **Use Automatic Tuning:** Leverage Oracle's automatic tuning features, such as Automatic Database Diagnostic Monitor (ADDM) and Automatic SQL Tuning.

2. Data Model Optimization:

- **Schema Design:** Ensure that the database schema is well-designed and normalized to minimize data redundancy and improve performance.
- **Partitioning:** Use table partitioning to improve query performance and manage large tables efficiently.

```sql
CREATE TABLE sales (
    sale_date DATE,
    amount NUMBER
)
PARTITION BY RANGE (sale_date) (
    PARTITION p1 VALUES LESS THAN (TO_DATE('2024-01-01', 'YYYY-MM-DD')),
    PARTITION p2 VALUES LESS THAN (TO_DATE('2025-01-01', 'YYYY-MM-DD'))
);
```

3. Parallel Execution:

- **Enable Parallel Execution:** Use parallel execution to improve the performance of large queries and data manipulation operations.

```sql
ALTER SESSION ENABLE PARALLEL DML;
```

14.6 Managing Database Performance Issues

Performance issues can arise due to various factors, including poorly optimized queries, resource contention, and configuration problems. Addressing these issues promptly is essential for maintaining optimal performance.

1. Identifying Performance Bottlenecks:

- **Use Performance Views:** Analyze Oracle performance views to identify bottlenecks and performance issues.

```
SELECT * FROM v$session_wait;
```

- **Analyze AWR Reports:** Review Automatic Workload Repository (AWR) reports to identify performance trends and problem areas.

2. Troubleshooting Techniques:

- **Check Wait Events:** Examine wait events to understand where the database is spending time and address underlying issues.

```
SELECT event, wait_time, time_waited
FROM v$session_wait
WHERE wait_time > 0;
```

- **Review Execution Plans:** Analyze query execution plans to identify inefficient operations and optimize queries.

3. **Performance Tuning Best Practices:**

- **Regular Maintenance:** Perform regular maintenance tasks such as analyzing tables, rebuilding indexes, and updating statistics.
- **Continuous Monitoring:** Continuously monitor database performance and adjust tuning strategies based on changing workloads and requirements.

14.7 Summary

In this chapter, we explored performance tuning and optimization techniques for Oracle Database, including understanding performance metrics, optimizing queries, managing resources, tuning database configurations, and addressing performance issues. Effective performance tuning enhances query performance, optimizes resource utilization, and ensures efficient operation of the database system.

By following these best practices and leveraging Oracle's performance tuning tools and features, you can achieve optimal performance and maintain a responsive and efficient database environment. In the next chapter, we will discuss advanced topics in Oracle Database, including advanced features, data warehousing, and emerging technologies.

Chapter 15: Advanced Features and Emerging Technologies

15.1 Introduction to Advanced Features

Oracle Database offers a range of advanced features designed to address complex requirements, improve performance, and enhance functionality. This chapter explores some of these advanced features and emerging technologies that can help you leverage Oracle Database's full potential.

15.2 Advanced Database Features

1. Oracle Real Application Clusters (RAC):

- **Overview:** Oracle RAC enables multiple instances of the Oracle Database to run on a cluster of servers, providing high availability and scalability.
- **Key Benefits:**
    - **High Availability:** Ensures continuous database availability even if one or more nodes fail.
    - **Scalability:** Allows you to scale out by adding more nodes to the cluster.
- **Configuration:**
    - **Install and Configure RAC:** Set up Oracle RAC using Oracle Clusterware and the Database Configuration Assistant (DBCA).

```
dbca -createDatabase
```

- **Monitor RAC Instances:** Use tools like Oracle Grid Infrastructure and Enterprise Manager to monitor RAC performance and manage instances.

2. Oracle Data Guard:

- **Overview:** Oracle Data Guard provides disaster recovery and data protection by maintaining one or more standby databases.
- **Key Benefits:**
    - **Disaster Recovery:** Provides automated failover and switchover capabilities to maintain database availability.
    - **Data Protection:** Ensures data is synchronized between primary and standby databases.
- **Configuration:**
    - **Create Data Guard Configuration:** Use the Data Guard Broker to configure and manage primary and standby databases.

    ```
    ALTER SYSTEM SET DG_BROKER_START = TRUE;
    ```

    - **Monitor Data Guard:** Use Oracle Enterprise Manager or Data Guard views to monitor and manage Data Guard environments.

3. Oracle Partitioning:

- **Overview:** Partitioning allows you to divide large tables and indexes into smaller, more manageable pieces, improving query performance and manageability.
- **Types of Partitioning:**
  - **Range Partitioning:** Divides data based on ranges of values.
  - **List Partitioning:** Divides data based on a list of values.
  - **Hash Partitioning:** Distributes data across a fixed number of partitions using a hash function.
- **Configuration:**
  - **Create Partitioned Table:** Define partitioning schemes when creating tables.

```sql
CREATE TABLE orders (
    order_id NUMBER,
    order_date DATE,
    amount NUMBER
)
PARTITION BY RANGE (order_date) (
    PARTITION p1 VALUES LESS THAN (TO_DATE('2024-01-01', 'YYYY-MM-DD')),
    PARTITION p2 VALUES LESS THAN (TO_DATE('2025-01-01', 'YYYY-MM-DD'))
);
```

4. Oracle Advanced Queuing (AQ):

- **Overview:** Oracle AQ provides messaging and queuing capabilities within the Oracle Database, enabling reliable message delivery and processing.
- **Key Benefits:**
  - **Message Reliability:** Ensures that messages are delivered and processed in the correct order.
  - **Integration:** Integrates with Oracle Database applications and other messaging systems.
- **Configuration:**
  - **Create Queues:** Define and manage queues and message types.

```
BEGIN
  DBMS_AQADM.CREATE_QUEUE_TABLE(
    queue_table => 'order_queue_table',
    queue_payload_type =>
'SYS.AQ$_JMS_TEXT_MESSAGE'
  );
  DBMS_AQADM.CREATE_QUEUE(
    queue_name => 'order_queue',
    queue_table => 'order_queue_table'
  );
  DBMS_AQADM.START_QUEUE(
    queue_name => 'order_queue'
  );
END;
```

5. Oracle Multitenant Architecture:

- **Overview:** Oracle Multitenant architecture enables a single Oracle Database instance to manage multiple databases (pluggable databases) within a single container database.
- **Key Benefits:**
    - **Consolidation:** Reduces overhead and simplifies management by consolidating multiple databases into a single container.
    - **Isolation:** Provides database isolation and resource management for each pluggable database.
- **Configuration:**
    - **Create Container and Pluggable Databases:** Use Database Configuration Assistant (DBCA) or SQL commands to create and manage container and pluggable databases.

```
CREATE DATABASE CDB1
CONTAINER = ALL;

CREATE PLUGGABLE DATABASE PDB1
ADMIN USER pdb_admin IDENTIFIED BY
password;
```

15.3 Emerging Technologies

1. Autonomous Database:

- **Overview:** Oracle Autonomous Database uses machine learning and automation to manage and

optimize database operations with minimal human intervention.
- **Key Benefits:**
  - **Self-Patching and Self-Tuning:** Automatically applies patches and tunes performance without manual intervention.
  - **Scalability:** Scales resources automatically based on workload demands.
- **Configuration:**
  - **Create Autonomous Database Instance:** Use Oracle Cloud Console or CLI to create and manage Autonomous Database instances.

```
oci db autonomous-database create --compartment-id <compartment_id> --db-name <db_name> --cpu-core-count <cores> --data-storage-size-in-tbs <size>
```

2. Oracle Machine Learning (OML):

- **Overview:** Oracle Machine Learning integrates machine learning algorithms and models directly into the Oracle Database, enabling advanced analytics and predictive modeling.
- **Key Benefits:**
  - **In-Database Analytics:** Perform machine learning and analytics directly within the database environment.
  - **Data Integration:** Leverage data stored in Oracle Database for training and deploying machine learning models.
- **Configuration:**

- **Use OML Packages:** Utilize Oracle Machine Learning packages and tools to develop and deploy machine learning models.

```
BEGIN
  DBMS_DATA_MINING.CREATE_MODEL(
    model_name => 'my_model',
    mining_function => 'CLASSIFICATION',
    data_table_name => 'training_data',
    target_column_name => 'target'
  );
END;
```

3. Blockchain Tables:

- **Overview:** Oracle Blockchain Tables provide tamper-evident and verifiable tables that store data in a secure and immutable manner.
- **Key Benefits:**
    - **Data Integrity:** Ensures data is immutable and verifiable, enhancing security and trustworthiness.
    - **Compliance:** Supports regulatory compliance by providing tamper-evidence.
- **Configuration:**
    - **Create Blockchain Table:** Define blockchain tables to store immutable records.

```
CREATE TABLE blockchain_table (
    id NUMBER PRIMARY KEY,
    data VARCHAR2(100),
    blockchain_table;
```

4. JSON and XML Support:

- **Overview:** Oracle Database offers robust support for JSON and XML data types, enabling efficient storage, querying, and manipulation of semi-structured data.
- **Key Benefits:**
    - **Flexible Data Storage:** Store and query JSON and XML data within the database.
    - **Integration:** Integrate JSON and XML data with relational data and applications.
- **Configuration:**
    - **Store and Query JSON Data:**

```
CREATE TABLE json_table (
    id NUMBER PRIMARY KEY,
    data CLOB CHECK (data IS JSON)
);

INSERT INTO json_table (id, data) VALUES (1, '{"name": "John", "age": 30}');

SELECT data->>'name' AS name FROM json_table;
```

- **Store and Query XML Data:**

```
CREATE TABLE xml_table (
    id NUMBER PRIMARY KEY,
    data XMLTYPE
);

INSERT INTO xml_table (id, data) VALUES (1,
XMLTYPE('<person><name>John</name><age>30</age></person>'));

SELECT data.extract('//name').getStringVal()
AS name FROM xml_table;
```

15.4 Best Practices for Advanced Features

1. Plan and Test:

- **Plan Implementations:** Carefully plan the implementation of advanced features based on your requirements and objectives.
- **Test Thoroughly:** Perform thorough testing in a development or staging environment before deploying to production.

2. Monitor and Optimize:

- **Monitor Performance:** Continuously monitor the performance of advanced features and optimize configurations as needed.

- **Adjust Resources:** Ensure that resources are allocated appropriately to support the advanced features effectively.

3. Stay Updated:

- **Keep Abreast of Updates:** Stay informed about new developments and updates related to advanced features and emerging technologies.
- **Upgrade Regularly:** Regularly upgrade to newer versions of Oracle Database to take advantage of new features and improvements.

15.5 Summary

In this chapter, we explored advanced features of Oracle Database, including Oracle RAC, Data Guard, partitioning, Advanced Queuing, Multitenant architecture, and emerging technologies such as Autonomous Database, Machine Learning, Blockchain Tables, and JSON/XML support. We also discussed best practices for implementing and managing these features to enhance your database environment.

By leveraging these advanced features and staying current with emerging technologies, you can maximize the capabilities of Oracle Database, improve performance, and address complex business requirements. In the next chapter, we will delve into database administration best practices, focusing on effective management and maintenance strategies for Oracle Database.

Chapter 16: Database Administration Best Practices

16.1 Introduction to Database Administration

Database administration involves managing and maintaining the Oracle Database to ensure its optimal performance, security, and reliability. Effective database administration is critical for ensuring that the database environment meets organizational needs and operates smoothly. This chapter covers best practices for database administration, including backup and recovery, security management, performance tuning, and routine maintenance.

16.2 Backup and Recovery

1. Importance of Backup and Recovery:

- **Data Protection:** Regular backups protect against data loss due to hardware failures, software issues, or user errors.
- **Disaster Recovery:** Enables recovery of the database to a specific point in time in case of a disaster.

2. Backup Types:

- **Full Backup:** A complete backup of the entire database, including all data files, control files, and archived redo logs.

```
RMAN> BACKUP DATABASE PLUS ARCHIVELOG;
```

- **Incremental Backup:** Backs up only the changes made since the last backup. This reduces backup time and storage requirements.

> RMAN> BACKUP INCREMENTAL LEVEL 1 DATABASE;

- **Differential Backup:** Backs up changes made since the last full backup.

3. **Backup Strategies:**

    - **Regular Scheduling:** Schedule regular backups to ensure data is consistently protected.

> RMAN> CONFIGURE BACKUP OPTIMIZATION ON;

   - **Offsite Storage:** Store backups in offsite locations or cloud storage to protect against site-specific disasters.
   - **Testing Backups:** Regularly test backups by performing restore operations to ensure they are valid and usable.

4. **Recovery Techniques:**

    - **Point-in-Time Recovery:** Recover the database to a specific point in time using archived redo logs.

```
RMAN> RECOVER DATABASE UNTIL TIME 'YYYY-MM-DD HH24:MI:SS';
```

- **Restore and Recovery:** Use RMAN or manual methods to restore and recover the database from backup files.

```
RMAN> RESTORE DATABASE;
RMAN> RECOVER DATABASE;
```

16.3 Security Management

1. User and Role Management:

- **Create and Manage Users:** Create database users with appropriate privileges and roles.

```
CREATE USER john IDENTIFIED BY password;
GRANT CONNECT, RESOURCE TO john;
```

- **Implement Roles:** Use roles to group and manage privileges more efficiently.

```
CREATE ROLE analyst;
GRANT SELECT ON employees TO analyst;
GRANT analyst TO john;
```

- **Privilege Management:** Assign only necessary privileges to users and roles, following the principle of least privilege.

2. **Data Encryption:**

- **Transparent Data Encryption (TDE):** Encrypt sensitive data stored in the database to protect it from unauthorized access.

```
ALTER TABLE employees ADD (salary ENCRYPT);
```

- **Network Encryption:** Encrypt data transmitted between the database and clients using Oracle Advanced Security.

```
ALTER SYSTEM SET SQLNET.ENCRYPTION_CLIENT = required;
ALTER SYSTEM SET SQLNET.ENCRYPTION_TYPES_CLIENT = (AES256);
```

3. **Auditing and Compliance:**

- **Enable Auditing:** Configure auditing to track database activities and user actions.

```
AUDIT ALL BY john BY ACCESS;
```

- **Monitor and Review:** Regularly review audit logs and reports to detect and address security issues.

4. Vulnerability Management:

- **Patch Management:** Regularly apply security patches and updates to address vulnerabilities.

```
opatch lsinventory
opatch apply
```

- **Security Configurations:** Implement security best practices, such as disabling unused features and services.

16.4 Performance Tuning

1. Monitoring Performance:

- **Use Oracle Enterprise Manager (OEM):** Monitor database performance metrics and receive alerts for performance issues.
- **Analyze Performance Views:** Review performance views to identify bottlenecks and resource usage.

```
SELECT * FROM v$session;
SELECT * FROM v$system_event;
```

2. Optimizing Queries:

- **Review Execution Plans:** Analyze and optimize query execution plans to improve performance.

```
EXPLAIN PLAN FOR
SELECT * FROM orders WHERE order_date = SYSDATE;
```

- **Index Management:** Create and maintain indexes to speed up query performance.

```
CREATE INDEX idx_order_date ON orders(order_date);
```

3. Resource Management:

- **Manage Memory:** Tune memory parameters such as SGA and PGA to optimize performance.

```
ALTER SYSTEM SET SGA_TARGET = 1G;

ALTER SYSTEM SET PGA_AFFREGATE_TARGET=512M;
```

Manage CPU Resources: Use Oracle Resource Manager to allocate CPU resources effectively.

```
BEGIN
  DBMS_RESOURCE_MANAGER.CREATE_PLAN(
    PLAN => 'cpu_plan',
    COMMENTS => 'CPU resource management plan'
  );
END;
```

16.5 Routine Maintenance

1. Regular Maintenance Tasks:

- **Analyze and Optimize Tables:** Regularly analyze and optimize tables to maintain performance.

```
ANALYZE TABLE employees COMPUTE STATISTICS;
```

- **Rebuild Indexes:** Rebuild indexes periodically to reduce fragmentation.

```
ALTER INDEX idx_employee REBUILD;
```

- **Monitor and Clean Up:** Monitor database growth and clean up obsolete or unused data.

2. Database Health Checks:

- **Check Data Integrity:** Perform regular checks to ensure data integrity and consistency.

```
DBMS_REPAIR.CHECK_OBJECT(OBJECT_NAME =>
'employees');
```

- **Review Configuration:** Periodically review and adjust database configurations based on performance metrics and workload changes.

16.6 Backup and Recovery Best Practices

- **Document Procedures:** Document backup and recovery procedures and ensure they are up-to-date.
- **Automate Backups:** Use automated tools and scripts to perform regular backups and minimize manual intervention.
- **Implement Backup Verification:** Regularly verify backups to ensure they can be restored successfully.

16.7 Security Management Best Practices

- **Regularly Review User Privileges:** Periodically review and adjust user privileges to ensure they align with current roles and responsibilities.
- **Enforce Strong Password Policies:** Implement and enforce strong password policies to enhance security.
- **Conduct Security Audits:** Regularly conduct security audits to identify and address potential vulnerabilities.

16.8 Performance Tuning Best Practices

- **Use Monitoring Tools:** Utilize monitoring tools to continuously track performance and identify areas for improvement.
- **Prioritize Performance Issues:** Address performance issues based on their impact on critical applications and operations.
- **Stay Updated on Best Practices:** Stay informed about best practices and updates related to performance tuning and optimization.

16.9 Summary

In this chapter, we covered best practices for database administration, including backup and recovery, security management, performance tuning, and routine maintenance. Effective database administration ensures data protection, security, and optimal performance, contributing to a stable and efficient database environment.

By following these best practices, you can effectively manage and maintain your Oracle Database, addressing key aspects of backup, security, performance, and routine maintenance. In the next chapter, we will explore database automation and DevOps practices, focusing on tools and techniques to streamline database management and integration with modern development workflows.

Chapter 17: Database Automation and DevOps Practices

17.1 Introduction to Database Automation

Database automation involves using tools and techniques to streamline and manage database operations, reducing manual intervention and minimizing errors. Automation is a critical component in modern database management, enhancing efficiency, consistency, and reliability. DevOps practices, which integrate development and operations, further extend automation to improve collaboration, continuous integration, and deployment processes.

17.2 Database Automation Tools and Techniques

1. Oracle Enterprise Manager (OEM):

- **Overview:** Oracle Enterprise Manager provides a comprehensive suite of tools for database management, including automation features.
- **Key Features:**
    - **Automated Monitoring:** Automatically monitors database performance and alerts administrators to potential issues.
    - **Automated Patching:** Streamlines the process of applying patches and updates.

```
# Apply a patch using OEM
emcli patch apply -patch_id=<patch_id>
```

- **Configuration:**
  - **Set Up Monitoring:** Configure automated monitoring and alerting for performance and availability.

```
EXEC DBMS_SCHEDULER.create_job(
   job_name => 'CHECK_DB_HEALTH',
   job_type => 'PLSQL_BLOCK',
   job_action => 'BEGIN dbms_monitor.run; END;',
   start_date => SYSTIMESTAMP,
   repeat_interval => 'FREQ=DAILY; BYHOUR=2'
);
```

2. Oracle Automatic Storage Management (ASM):

- **Overview:** Oracle ASM automates the management of database storage, including disk space allocation and file placement.
- **Key Features:**
  - **Automatic Storage Management:** Handles disk groups and storage operations without manual intervention.
  - **Performance Optimization:** Optimizes I/O performance and balances storage across disks.
- **Configuration:**
  - **Create Disk Groups:** Use SQL commands to configure ASM disk groups.

```
CREATE DISKGROUP data EXTERNAL
REDUNDANCY DISK '/dev/sd*';
```

3. Oracle Data Guard Broker:

- **Overview:** Data Guard Broker automates the management and configuration of Oracle Data Guard environments for high availability and disaster recovery.
- **Key Features:**
    - **Automated Failover:** Automatically handles failover and switchover operations.
    - **Configuration Management:** Simplifies the configuration and monitoring of Data Guard setups.
- **Configuration:**
    - **Configure Data Guard Broker:** Use Data Guard Broker commands to manage and monitor Data Guard environments.

```
ALTER SYSTEM SET DG_BROKER_START =
TRUE;
```

4. Oracle RMAN (Recovery Manager):

- **Overview:** RMAN automates backup and recovery tasks, simplifying the backup process and ensuring data protection.
- **Key Features:**
    - **Automated Backups:** Schedule and automate backup operations.

- **Backup Validation:** Automatically validates backups to ensure integrity.

```
# Schedule RMAN backup
rman target / <<EOF
BACKUP DATABASE PLUS ARCHIVELOG;
EOF
```

- **Configuration:**
  - **Configure Backup Schedules:** Use RMAN scripts or Oracle Scheduler to automate backup operations.

```
BEGIN
  DBMS_SCHEDULER.create_job(
    job_name => 'BACKUP_JOB',
    job_type => 'EXECUTABLE',
    job_action => '/path/to/rman_script.sh',
    start_date => SYSTIMESTAMP,
    repeat_interval => 'FREQ=DAILY; BYHOUR=2'
  );
END;
```

17.3 DevOps Practices for Database Management

1. Infrastructure as Code (IaC):

- **Overview:** IaC involves managing database infrastructure through code, enabling automated

provisioning, configuration, and management of database environments.
- **Key Tools:**
    - **Terraform:** Automates the creation and management of database infrastructure.

    ```hcl
    Copy code
    resource "oci_database_db_system" "example" {
      compartment_id = "your_compartment_id"
      ...
    }
    ```

    - **Ansible:** Automates configuration and management tasks for database environments.

    ```
    - name: Install Oracle Database
      hosts: db_servers
      tasks:
        - name: Install Oracle Database
          yum:
            name: oracle-database
            state: present
    ```

2. Continuous Integration and Continuous Deployment (CI/CD):

- **Overview:** CI/CD practices involve integrating database changes into development workflows and automating deployments.
- **Key Tools:**
    - **Jenkins:** Automates the build and deployment process for database applications.

    ```groovy
    Copy code
    pipeline {
      agent any
      stages {
        stage('Build') {
          steps {
            sh 'mvn clean package'
          }
        }
        stage('Deploy') {
          steps {
            sh 'deploy_script.sh'
          }
        }
      }
    }
    ```

    -
    -
    -

- **Liquibase:** Manages database schema changes and integrates with CI/CD pipelines.

```xml
<changeSet author="author" id="1">
<createTable tableName="employees">
    <column name="id" type="NUMBER">
      <constraints primaryKey="true"/>
    </column>
    <column name="name" type="VARCHAR2(100)"/>
  </createTable>
</changeSet>
```

3. Automated Testing:

- **Overview:** Automated testing ensures database changes are validated and do not introduce issues.
- **Key Tools:**
    - **SQL Developer:** Automates database testing and validation.

```
BEGIN
   dbms_sqltune.create_task(task_name => 'test_task', sql_id => 'your_sql_id');
END;
```

- **UTPLSQL:** Provides automated unit testing for PL/SQL code.

```
BEGIN
  ut.run('test_package');
END;
```

4. Monitoring and Logging:

- **Overview:** Automated monitoring and logging ensure that database performance and health are continuously tracked.
- **Key Tools:**
    - **Oracle Enterprise Manager (OEM):** Provides comprehensive monitoring and alerting capabilities.
    - **Grafana and Prometheus:** Monitor database metrics and visualize performance data.

```
scrape_configs:
  - job_name: 'oracle'
    static_configs:
      - targets: ['localhost:9090']
```

5. Automated Provisioning and Scaling:

- **Overview:** Automated provisioning and scaling ensure that database environments can dynamically adjust to workload changes.
- **Key Tools:**
    - **Oracle Cloud Infrastructure (OCI):** Provides automated provisioning and scaling features for cloud-based databases.

```
oci db autonomous-database create --
compartment-id <compartment_id> --db-
name <db_name> --cpu-core-count <cores> -
-data-storage-size-in-tbs <size>
```

- **Configuration:**
  - **Define Scaling Policies:** Configure scaling policies based on workload requirements.

```
oci autoscale auto-scaling-config create --
compartment-id <compartment_id> --
display-name <config_name> --min-capacity
<min> --max-capacity <max>
```

17.4 Best Practices for Database Automation and DevOps

1. Standardize Processes:

- **Document Procedures:** Document automated processes and configurations to ensure consistency and clarity.
- **Use Templates:** Create reusable templates for common tasks to streamline automation.

2. Test Automation:

- **Validate Automation Scripts:** Thoroughly test automation scripts and configurations in a staging environment before deployment.

- **Monitor Automation:** Continuously monitor automated processes to ensure they operate as expected.

3. Integrate with DevOps Pipelines:

- **Automate Deployments:** Integrate database changes into CI/CD pipelines to automate deployments and ensure smooth transitions.
- **Coordinate with Development:** Ensure coordination between development and operations teams for seamless integration.

4. Ensure Security and Compliance:

- **Automate Security Checks:** Implement automated security checks and audits to ensure compliance with policies and regulations.
- **Review and Update:** Regularly review and update automation practices to address evolving security and compliance requirements.

17.5 Summary

In this chapter, we explored database automation and DevOps practices, including tools and techniques for automating database management tasks, integrating with CI/CD pipelines, and managing infrastructure as code. We discussed best practices for implementing automation and DevOps to enhance efficiency, collaboration, and reliability in database management. By leveraging automation and DevOps practices, you can streamline database operations, reduce manual intervention, and improve the overall management of your Oracle Database environment. In the next chapter, we will delve into emerging trends and future directions in database technology, focusing on innovations and advancements shaping the future of database management.

Chapter 18: Emerging Trends and Future Directions in Database Technology

18.1 Introduction

The landscape of database technology is constantly evolving, driven by advancements in hardware, software, and data management practices. This chapter explores emerging trends and future directions in database technology, including innovations that are shaping the future of database management. Understanding these trends will help you stay ahead in the field and leverage new technologies to enhance your database environment.

18.2 Emerging Trends in Database Technology

1. Cloud Databases:

- **Overview:** Cloud databases are becoming increasingly popular as organizations move their data and applications to cloud environments. They offer scalability, flexibility, and cost-efficiency compared to traditional on-premises databases.
- **Key Features:**
    - **Scalability:** Easily scale resources up or down based on workload demands.
    - **Managed Services:** Leverage managed database services that handle maintenance, backups, and updates.
- **Examples:**
    - **Amazon Aurora:** A fully managed relational database compatible with MySQL and PostgreSQL.

- - **Oracle Autonomous Database:** An automated cloud database that handles provisioning, patching, and tuning.

2. Multi-Cloud and Hybrid Cloud Deployments:

- **Overview:** Multi-cloud and hybrid cloud strategies involve using multiple cloud providers or combining cloud and on-premises environments to meet business needs.
- **Key Benefits:**
  - **Flexibility:** Avoid vendor lock-in and choose the best services from different providers.
  - **Disaster Recovery:** Enhance disaster recovery capabilities by distributing data across multiple clouds.
- **Challenges:**
  - **Data Integration:** Manage and integrate data across diverse environments.
  - **Security:** Ensure consistent security policies across multiple cloud providers.

3. Data Privacy and Security:

- **Overview:** As data breaches and privacy concerns grow, ensuring robust data privacy and security measures is crucial.
- **Key Practices:**
  - **Data Encryption:** Encrypt data both at rest and in transit to protect it from unauthorized access.

- - **Access Controls:** Implement fine-grained access controls to restrict data access based on roles and permissions.
- **Regulations:**
  - **GDPR:** The General Data Protection Regulation mandates strict data protection measures for EU citizens.
  - **CCPA:** The California Consumer Privacy Act provides privacy rights and consumer protection for residents of California.

4. Artificial Intelligence (AI) and Machine Learning (ML):

- **Overview:** AI and ML are being integrated into database management systems to enhance performance, automate tasks, and provide advanced analytics.
- **Applications:**
  - **Predictive Analytics:** Use ML algorithms to analyze data and predict future trends.
  - **Automated Tuning:** Implement AI-driven performance tuning to optimize database operations.
- **Examples:**
  - **Oracle Machine Learning:** Integrates ML capabilities into Oracle Database for in-database analytics.
  - **Google BigQuery ML:** Allows users to build and deploy ML models directly within BigQuery.

5. Blockchain Technology:

- **Overview:** Blockchain technology provides a decentralized and immutable ledger for recording transactions, offering new possibilities for data management and security.
- **Applications:**
  - **Supply Chain Management:** Track and verify transactions across supply chains to ensure authenticity and transparency.
  - **Smart Contracts:** Automate contract execution and enforcement through programmable transactions.
- **Examples:**
  - **Oracle Blockchain Platform:** Provides a secure and scalable blockchain solution for enterprises.

6. NoSQL and NewSQL Databases:

- **Overview:** NoSQL and NewSQL databases offer alternatives to traditional relational databases, addressing specific needs such as scalability, flexibility, and real-time processing.
- **NoSQL Databases:**
  - **Document Stores:** Store and manage semi-structured data (e.g., MongoDB, Couchbase).
  - **Key-Value Stores:** Handle high-throughput, low-latency access to key-value pairs (e.g., Redis, Riak).
- **NewSQL Databases:**
  - **Overview:** Provide the scalability of NoSQL databases while maintaining ACID (Atomicity,

Consistency, Isolation, Durability) properties of traditional SQL databases (e.g., Google Spanner, CockroachDB).

18.3 Future Directions in Database Technology

1. Autonomous Databases:

- **Overview:** Autonomous databases use AI and automation to manage database operations, reducing the need for human intervention.
- **Future Developments:**
    - **Enhanced Automation:** Further advancements in AI will drive more sophisticated automation for provisioning, tuning, and security.
    - **Self-Healing Capabilities:** Development of self-healing databases that can automatically detect and correct issues without human intervention.

2. Edge Computing:

- **Overview:** Edge computing involves processing data closer to its source, reducing latency and improving performance for real-time applications.
- **Future Trends:**
    - **Distributed Databases:** Implement databases that support edge computing environments, allowing for data processing and storage at the edge.

- o **IoT Integration:** Enhance support for Internet of Things (IoT) devices and applications through edge databases.

3. Quantum Computing:

- **Overview:** Quantum computing has the potential to revolutionize data processing and analysis by leveraging quantum mechanics to solve complex problems.
- **Future Applications:**
  - o **Complex Analytics:** Perform complex data analysis and optimization that are currently impractical with classical computers.
  - o **Cryptography:** Develop new cryptographic methods to enhance data security.

4. Data Fabric and Data Mesh:

- **Overview:** Data fabric and data mesh concepts aim to create a unified and decentralized approach to data management.
- **Data Fabric:**
  - o **Overview:** Provides a cohesive and integrated view of data across various sources and environments.
  - o **Future Trends:** Enhance data integration and management through advanced data fabric technologies.
- **Data Mesh:**
  - o **Overview:** Emphasizes a decentralized approach to data management, where data

ownership and responsibility are distributed across domains.
- **Future Trends:** Implement data mesh architectures to improve scalability and agility in data management.

18.4 Preparing for the Future

1. Stay Informed:

- **Industry Trends:** Keep up-to-date with the latest trends and advancements in database technology through industry publications, conferences, and webinars.
- **Continuous Learning:** Invest in ongoing education and training to stay current with new technologies and best practices.

2. Embrace Innovation:

- **Pilot New Technologies:** Experiment with emerging technologies in test environments to evaluate their potential benefits and impact on your organization.
- **Adopt Best Practices:** Implement best practices for data management, security, and performance to ensure a successful transition to new technologies.

3. Plan for Change:

- **Strategic Planning:** Develop a strategic plan for adopting new technologies and integrating them into your existing database environment.

- **Change Management:** Implement change management processes to ensure a smooth transition and minimize disruptions during technology upgrades.

18.5 Summary

In this chapter, we explored emerging trends and future directions in database technology, including cloud databases, multi-cloud and hybrid cloud deployments, data privacy and security, AI and ML integration, blockchain technology, and NoSQL and NewSQL databases. We also discussed future directions such as autonomous databases, edge computing, quantum computing, and data fabric/data mesh concepts.

By staying informed and embracing innovation, you can effectively prepare for the future of database technology and leverage new advancements to enhance your database environment. In the next chapter, we will provide a comprehensive review and summary of key concepts covered throughout the book, offering insights into best practices and actionable takeaways for mastering Oracle Database.

Chapter 19: Review and Summary: Mastering Oracle Database

19.1 Introduction

In this concluding chapter, we review the key concepts covered throughout the book and summarize the best practices and actionable insights for mastering Oracle Database. Our goal is to consolidate your learning and provide a roadmap for applying the knowledge gained to effectively manage and optimize your Oracle Database environment.

19.2 Recap of Key Concepts

1. Understanding Oracle Database Architecture:

- **Instance and Database Architecture:** We explored the fundamental components of Oracle Database, including instances, databases, and their interactions. Understanding these components is crucial for effective database management and troubleshooting.
    - **Instance:** Consists of memory structures and background processes.
    - **Database:** Includes data files, control files, and redo log files.
- **Data Storage Structures:** We discussed the various storage structures, such as tablespaces, data files, and segments, which are essential for data organization and management.

2. Database Design and Normalization:

- **Data Modeling:** We covered the principles of data modeling, including entity-relationship diagrams (ERDs) and normalization, to design efficient and effective database schemas.
    - **Normalization:** Process of organizing data to minimize redundancy and improve data integrity.
    - **Denormalization:** Sometimes used for performance optimization by reducing the complexity of joins.
- **Schema Design:** Best practices for designing schemas that support data integrity, scalability, and performance.

3. SQL and PL/SQL Programming:

- **SQL Basics:** We reviewed the core SQL concepts, including queries, joins, and aggregations, which are fundamental for interacting with the database.
    - **SELECT, INSERT, UPDATE, DELETE:** Core SQL operations for data manipulation.
    - **Joins:** Combining data from multiple tables.
- **PL/SQL Programming:** We explored PL/SQL, Oracle's procedural extension to SQL, for writing complex queries, procedures, functions, and triggers.
    - **Procedures and Functions:** Used for encapsulating logic and enhancing reusability.
    - **Triggers:** Automated responses to database events.

4. Backup and Recovery:

- **Backup Types:** We covered various backup types (full, incremental, differential) and their importance for data protection.
    - **RMAN:** Oracle's Recovery Manager for automating backup and recovery tasks.
- **Recovery Techniques:** We discussed point-in-time recovery, restore and recovery procedures, and best practices for ensuring data integrity and availability.

5. Database Administration Best Practices:

- **Security Management:** Best practices for managing user roles, data encryption, and access controls to secure the database environment.
    - **Oracle Enterprise Manager (OEM):** Tools for monitoring and managing security.
- **Performance Tuning:** Techniques for optimizing database performance, including query optimization, index management, and resource management.
    - **Execution Plans:** Analyzing and optimizing SQL execution plans.

6. Database Automation and DevOps Practices:

- **Automation Tools:** We reviewed tools and techniques for automating database management tasks, including Oracle Enterprise Manager, RMAN, and Data Guard Broker.
    - **Infrastructure as Code (IaC):** Automating infrastructure management using tools like Terraform and Ansible.

- **CI/CD Integration:** Best practices for integrating database changes into CI/CD pipelines and automating deployments.

7. Emerging Trends and Future Directions:

- **Cloud Databases:** The rise of cloud databases, multi-cloud and hybrid cloud deployments, and their benefits for scalability and flexibility.
    - **Autonomous Databases:** AI-driven databases that automate management tasks.
- **AI and ML Integration:** The impact of artificial intelligence and machine learning on database management and performance optimization.
    - **Predictive Analytics:** Using ML algorithms for data analysis and forecasting.
- **Blockchain Technology:** Applications of blockchain for secure and transparent data management.

19.3 Best Practices for Mastering Oracle Database

1. Continuous Learning and Professional Development:

- **Certifications and Training:** Pursue certifications such as Oracle Certified Professional (OCP) and stay updated with the latest Oracle technologies and best practices.
- **Community Engagement:** Participate in Oracle user groups, forums, and conferences to stay connected with the community and learn from peers.

2. Implementing Best Practices:

- **Documentation:** Maintain thorough documentation of database configurations, procedures, and best practices to ensure consistency and facilitate troubleshooting.
- **Automation:** Leverage automation tools and scripts to streamline routine tasks and reduce manual intervention.
- **Regular Reviews:** Periodically review and update database configurations, security policies, and performance settings to adapt to changing requirements and technologies.

3. Planning and Strategy:

- **Capacity Planning:** Perform regular capacity planning to ensure that your database environment can handle current and future workloads.
- **Disaster Recovery Planning:** Develop and test disaster recovery plans to ensure that you can quickly recover from data loss or system failures.

4. Embracing Innovation:

- **Pilot New Technologies:** Experiment with emerging technologies and trends in test environments before deploying them in production.
- **Evaluate Impact:** Assess the impact of new technologies on your database environment and adjust strategies accordingly.

19.4 Actionable Takeaways

1. Review Key Concepts Regularly:

- Revisit key topics such as database architecture, SQL and PL/SQL programming, backup and recovery, and performance tuning to reinforce your understanding.

2. Apply Best Practices:

- Implement best practices for database design, administration, security, and performance to optimize your database environment.

3. Stay Updated:

- Keep abreast of emerging trends and technologies to leverage new advancements and stay competitive in the field.

4. Continuously Improve:

- Seek feedback, learn from experiences, and continuously improve your database management practices.

19.5 Conclusion

Mastering Oracle Database involves a deep understanding of its architecture, effective management practices, and staying current with emerging trends and technologies. By applying the knowledge and best practices covered in this book, you can enhance your skills, optimize database performance, and contribute to the success of your organization.

As you continue your journey with Oracle Database, remember that ongoing learning, adaptation, and innovation are key to mastering this powerful technology and staying at the forefront of the database management field.

Chapter 20: Case Studies and Real-World Applications

20.1 Introduction

In this final chapter, we explore real-world case studies and applications of Oracle Database to illustrate how the concepts and techniques discussed throughout the book are applied in practical scenarios. These case studies highlight different industries and use cases, demonstrating how Oracle Database can be leveraged to solve complex challenges and drive business success.

20.2 Case Study 1: Financial Services – Enhancing Transaction Processing

Background:

A major financial institution needed to improve the efficiency and scalability of its transaction processing system to handle a growing volume of transactions and meet regulatory requirements. The existing system faced performance bottlenecks and difficulties in managing large amounts of data.

Solution:

- **Database Architecture:** The institution adopted Oracle Exadata, a high-performance database machine designed for transaction processing and data warehousing.

- **Implementation:**
    - **High-Performance Storage:** Utilized Oracle Exadata's flash storage and smart scan features to accelerate data retrieval and processing.
    - **Automated Tuning:** Implemented Oracle Automatic Database Diagnostic Monitor (ADDM) and Oracle SQL Tuning Advisor to automatically identify and resolve performance issues.

    ```sql
    -- View ADDM recommendations
    SELECT * FROM DBA_ADVISOR_FINDINGS WHERE ADVISOR_NAME = 'ADDM';
    ```

    - **Data Compression:** Used Advanced Compression to reduce storage requirements and improve I/O performance.

    ```sql
    ALTER TABLE transactions COMPRESS FOR OLTP;
    ```

- **Outcome:**
    - **Improved Performance:** Achieved significant improvements in transaction processing speed and reduced response times.
    - **Scalability:** Enhanced the system's ability to scale with increasing transaction volumes, meeting regulatory compliance requirements.

20.3 Case Study 2: E-Commerce – Optimizing Customer Experience

Background:

An e-commerce company wanted to enhance the customer experience by improving the performance of its online store and providing personalized recommendations. The company faced challenges with slow query performance and difficulty in handling large amounts of customer data.

Solution:

- **Database Design:** The company redesigned its database schema to optimize performance and support advanced analytics.
- **Implementation:**
    - **Data Warehousing:** Implemented Oracle Database's data warehousing capabilities to aggregate and analyze customer data.

    ```
    CREATE MATERIALIZED VIEW customer_summary AS
    SELECT customer_id, COUNT(order_id) AS order_count, SUM(order_amount) AS total_spent
    FROM orders
    GROUP BY customer_id;
    ```

    - **Indexing:** Added indexes to frequently queried columns to speed up query performance.

```sql
CREATE INDEX idx_customer_id ON
orders(customer_id);
```

- **Personalization:** Utilized Oracle Machine Learning to develop recommendation algorithms based on customer behavior and preferences.

```sql
BEGIN
  dbms_data_mining.create_model(
    model_name =>
'customer_recommendations',
    ...
  );
END;
```

- **Outcome:**
    - **Enhanced Performance:** Reduced query response times and improved the overall performance of the online store.
    - **Personalized Recommendations:** Increased customer satisfaction by providing personalized product recommendations based on browsing and purchase history.

20.4 Case Study 3: Healthcare – Ensuring Data Security and Compliance

Background:

A healthcare provider needed to enhance the security and compliance of its electronic health record (EHR) system to meet stringent regulatory requirements and protect sensitive patient data.

Solution:

- **Security Measures:** Implemented Oracle Database's advanced security features to safeguard patient information and ensure compliance with healthcare regulations.
- **Implementation:**
    - **Data Encryption:** Used Transparent Data Encryption (TDE) to encrypt sensitive data stored in the database.

    ```
    ALTER SYSTEM SET ENCRYPTION KEY
    IDENTIFIED BY 'your_password';
    ALTER TABLE patients ENCRYPT;
    ```

    - **Access Controls:** Implemented fine-grained access controls and Oracle Label Security to restrict access to sensitive data based on user roles and data labels.

```
BEGIN
  DBMS_RLS.ADD_POLICY(
    object_schema => 'healthcare',
    object_name => 'patients',
    policy_name => 'access_policy',
    function_schema => 'security',
    policy_function => 'secure_access'
  );
END;
```

- **Audit Trails:** Enabled auditing to track access and modifications to sensitive data.

```
AUDIT SELECT, INSERT, UPDATE, DELETE ON patients BY ACCESS;
```

- **Outcome:**
    - **Enhanced Security:** Achieved compliance with healthcare regulations and improved data protection measures.
    - **Auditability:** Improved the ability to monitor and review access to sensitive patient data, ensuring accountability and transparency.

20.5 Case Study 4: Telecommunications – Managing Network Data

Background:

A telecommunications company needed to manage and analyze vast amounts of network data to improve service quality and optimize network performance. The company faced challenges with data integration and real-time analytics.

Solution:

- **Data Integration:** Used Oracle Data Integrator (ODI) to integrate and transform data from various sources into a unified view.
- **Implementation:**
    - **ETL Processes:** Developed ETL (Extract, Transform, Load) processes to aggregate network performance data and generate real-time reports.

    ```
    -- Example ETL process using ODI
    INSERT INTO network_performance
    (timestamp, metric, value)
    SELECT current_timestamp, metric, value
    FROM raw_network_data;
    ```

    - **Real-Time Analytics:** Implemented Oracle Streams and Oracle GoldenGate for real-time data replication and analytics.

```
-- Example setup for Oracle GoldenGate
EXEC DBMS_CAPTURE_ADM.START_CAPTURE('capture_name');
```

- **Data Visualization:** Utilized Oracle Analytics Cloud to create dashboards and visualizations for monitoring network performance.

```
-- Create a dashboard to visualize network metrics
CREATE DASHBOARD network_performance_dashboard;
```

- **Outcome:**
    - **Improved Network Performance:** Enhanced the ability to monitor and optimize network performance in real-time.
    - **Data Integration:** Achieved a unified view of network data, facilitating better decision-making and service quality improvements.

20.6 Conclusion

In this chapter, we examined real-world case studies that demonstrate the application of Oracle Database concepts and techniques across different industries. From enhancing transaction processing in financial services to optimizing customer experience in e-commerce, improving data security in healthcare, and managing network data in telecommunications, these case studies illustrate the versatility and power of Oracle Database in solving complex challenges.

By understanding these practical applications, you can gain valuable insights into how to leverage Oracle Database to address specific needs and drive business success in your own organization. As you continue to apply the knowledge and best practices covered in this book, remember that real-world experience and continuous learning are key to mastering database management and staying at the forefront of technological advancements.